Is India ready for gender neutral laws?

UDIT MALIK

and

AYUSHI RAGHUWANSHI

ISBN- 978-93-5361-292-4

Table of Contents

INTRODUCTION

Gender is not the same as sex, where sex denotes the biological characteristics of women and men, gender has more to it, gender is the definition which is constructed by the society. It is determined by the social and cultural roles assigned to them in the society. When the society assigns different roles according to the gender then there arises discrimination from the commonly held perception that there are social roles which suit one gender more than the other.

The need for gender neutrality arises right here when the discrimination takes ground. Gender neutrality is the concept which emphasizes that the society should not distinguish the roles according to the sex or gender. It emphasizes the equal treatment of both men and women without any sort of discrimination socially, legally, politically and economically.

The gender roles have existed in the Indian society mainly due to the patriarchal system rooted deeply since ages. The attitude and behavior of the society towards any person is determined by the gender.

From the pre-historic era to late 60s, the condition and status of women was quite bad. In the ancient India, epics and Puranas equated women with property. Manu dictated that a woman would be dependent on her father in childhood, on her husband in youth and when her lord is dead, to her sons. Leave equality apart, women were not even treated as human being, they were just commodities in the eyes of men by whom you can make your daily chores done. Women were victims of widespread illiteracy, segregation in the dark and dingy rooms in the name of purdah, forced child marriage, indeterminable widowhood, rigidity of fidelity and opposition to remarriage of widows turning many of them into prostitutes, polygamy, female infanticide, violence and force to follow Sati, and the complete denial of individuality.

But the thinking and the perspective of the world towards women started to change a little with time. The first leader of our free India, Pandit Jawaharlal Nehru said "You can tell the condition of a nation by looking at the status of its women". The fight for gender equality and women's status began in India in the 20th century. Western-educated leaders like Mahatma Gandhi and others initiated this struggle by stating that a woman is completely equal to a men in all the senses. During the struggle of independence, we have seen millions of women, educated and illiterate, housewives and widows, students and elderly, participated in India's freedom movement because of Gandhi's influence. Mahatma Gandhi, the father of this free nation in which we are living today, stood for women rights in the dark misty period when women were confined to their houses and children. He was having an absolute faith in inherent power of women, he emphasized it by saying- "complete emancipation of women and her equality with man is the final goal of our social development, whose realization no power on earth can prevent".

In India, women are always at an advantage because of our recent laws which provides them so much freedom. For instance, ladies have a separate ticket counter at almost every place. They have seats reserved in buses. In metros, they have a complete coach reserved for themselves in every train. All these and other benefits are provided to them for their safety and security.

But the question arises here is are women using the laws meant for their protection in a right way or misusing them against men. Not every women but some are actually using their right to take revenge from men and for personal gains. Innocent men and families have been victimised because of such misuse of women protection laws.

But, the roads of change is long and hard. When there were women like Vijaya Lakshmi Pandit- the first women (and the first Indian) president of the United Nations General Assembly, Savitribai Phule- started India's first school for girls, Kamaladevi Chattopadhyay- social activist and Indian freedom fighter, Captain Prem Mathur-the first woman pilot in India, Sarojini Naidu- the "Nightingale of India", Sucheta Kriplani- the first woman Chief Minister in India, Indira Priyadarshini Gandhi- to date, the only female Prime minister of India, Justice Anna Chandy- the first female judge in India, and the first woman in India too become a High Court judge, Captain Lakshmi sahgal- Indian independence revolutionary, Rani Lakshmibai- who don't know her, such a brave woman who led rebellion against the British, some women were still looked upon inferior and subordinate to men. Indira

Gandhi's rule as Prime Minister of India was a triumph for women in leadership, yet the nation under her rule was populated by hundreds of millions of impoverished women, whose lives changed remarkably little during her term. India was no less than the days when Goddess like Sita had to defend herself against her husband's accusations of unchastity, impure, infidelity and Goddess like Draupadi had no option to say no to her brother-in laws who were pulling off her saree in the court, when her husband lost her in a gamble. Women were an object for men then, and were still no less than an object.

Men have always been caged to the social roles and functions based on their sex. The basic human characteristics have been distinguished to be feminine and masculine. Men cannot even express the most beautiful human emotions because that is not expected of them, they cannot show their grief, sorrow and pain because that does not fit in the basic masculine traits. The gender roles have been so deeply ingrained that there is no aspect which is left untouched; everything has been categorized into being feminine and masculine.

There are different notions about embracing masculinity, many of which have led to a rampant increase in crimes like violence in the society and crimes against women. A study conducted by the ICRW or the International Center for Research on Women on gender roles in India in 2018 came up with the conclusion that men's sense of "masculinity" significantly affects preferences for sons as well as inclination for violence towards the intimate partner.

The Indian patriarchal society led to gender inequality on many faces, and the women of the nation continued to be suppressed by the men. This prompted in the rise of the concept of feminism which stood for the rights of the women and their upliftment. As a result of the worsening condition of the women a number of programmes and legislations have been enacted to take up their cause.

The traditional gender roles contributed significantly to social evils against women like domestic violence, sexual harassment, dowry demands, female infanticide, female feticide, etc. Due to the rise in such crimes different legislations came up to address the issue. Most significant change came up after the December 2012 gang-rape in New Delhi, which led to widespread protests across the nation. It is one of the landmark fights for women's rights in India. The criminal law (amendment) act 2013 brought about changes which were gender- specific and protected only women form the crime. The amendments were made in consonance with the demands of more stringent laws for protecting women made principally by the feminist pressure groups. Consequently no protection was given to the male counterpart in case of any such offence committed against them. The concept of women empowerment cannot be confused with gender equality.

All this eventually led to a commonly perceived notion that only women could be victims at the hands of the men. Thus the legislators failed to address the right of equal protection to men.

The laws of the country seek to maintain order and well being of the people in the society. Every law has a specific purpose to serve as it is enacted with some predefined objectives. All the legislations are governed by the law of the land, which is the Constitution of India. The Constitutional provisions provide a framework within which the legislators enact laws. The preamble of the constitution provides for social, economic and political justice to the citizens.

Article 14[1] provides the right to equality, stating that "The state shall not deny to any person equality before the law or the equal protection of the laws within the territory of India". Somewhere in an attempt to protect the women from the rising number of crime against them, the equal protection of the law has been forsaken. Men have not been given protection under the law for offences like domestic violence, sexual harassment, rape etc. The very basic fundamental right has been taken away by such omission on the part of the legislature.

Article 15[2] prohibits discrimination of any kind, it says, "the state shall not discriminate against any citizen on grounds only of religion, race, caste, sex, place of birth or any of them." Discrimination on any grounds is not permitted by the constitution then why only women have been entitled to protection in certain offences? The number of female victims is more but

---

[1]https://www.india.gov.in/sites/upload_files/npi/files/coi_part_full.pdf
[2]http://www.legislative.gov.in/sites/default/files/COI-updated-as-31072018.pdf

that cannot justify the fact of completely overlooking the number of male victims. They too fall prey to such offences and do not have a recourse to seek protection which is a discrimination against them on the basis of gender.

There are a number of international standards and global commitments which stand up for the cause of gender equality, India being a signatory to these international covenants. The Universal Declaration of Human Rights 1948[3], the International Covenant on Civil and Political Rights 1966 and the International Covenant On Economic, Social And Cultural Rights 1966; all these conventions uphold the rights of the individual and mark no discrimination on any basis. These covenants strongly stand up for the promotion of gender neutral laws on every aspect.

---

[3] https://www.un.org/en/universal-declaration-human-rights/

India has however not succeeded in ensuring gender neutral laws on every aspect. Where most of the civil and criminal laws do not make a distinction of the victim on the basis of gender there are some laws which protect only women. the immoral traffic (prevention) act 1956, The dowry prohibition act 1961(amended in 1986), The indecent representation of women (prohibition) act 1986, The commission of sati (prevention) act 1987, Protection of women from domestic violence act 2005, The sexual harassment of women at workplace (prevention, prohibition and redressal) act 2013[4], The criminal law (amendment) act, 2013 to mention a few.

Let us see the whole aspect through this book.

---

[4]http://legislative.gov.in/actsofparliamentfromtheyear/sexual-harassment-women-workplace-prevention-prohibition-and-redressal

15

ORIGIN

A study into the traditional background of the society leads to clear understanding of the present needs of the society. The need for gender neutral laws in India too can be well comprehended by an insight into the history of the gender roles and their position in the society. The gender roles which have traditionally continued to exist over centuries in India have led to many social issues one of the prominent amongst which is gender discrimination.

Indian society has always been patriarchal in nature, a male dominated society where females have been relegated to a secondary or inferior position. The male members of the family and the society dominate every aspect of life.

Patriarchy has its roots deeply imbedded in the Indian society since ages. The commonly held belief has been that men are born to dominate and control while women are subordinate. Men and women have not been treated equally, the world has always belonged to men. Women are subjected to subordination; men are thought to be born superior to women. Women are always given secondary and inferior status in the family as well as the society.

The condition of women kept deteriorating with time especially after the foreign invasions. Social evils crept in the society which found their base in the patriarchal system. The marginalized role of women has particularly been due to the subordination and discrimination that they have faced over years. The women have been chained to superstitions, false beliefs and conventional norms set by the society. Their roles have been defined by the society and they are not allowed to act beyond the conventional role assigned to them. Though they too are born as individuals with human rights but they do not really have the rights. All the decisions which directly affect their life are taken by the male members of the family; they have no right to participate. Their life is restricted to domestic realm which includes only the household chores, raising up children and looking after the needs of the family. While men on the other hand have all the powers and a complete say in the matters of the society.

Women have been discriminated on every front of life; from basic necessities like food, education, property, employment etc to being a participant in the mainstream of the society. Women are expected to submit to the wishes of the family and devote their lives for the family. They are not considered individuals and are always identified as being associated to the male counterpart. Their identity lies in being someone's daughter, sister, wife, mother, etc,

A woman cannot have her dreams and aspirations in life, as in a patriarchy she first submits to her father's will and later to her husband's. In a patriarchal system a woman is not considered to be a separate and independent identity. Women have been facing injustice, subjugation, exploitation, oppression etc due to the prevalence of this system. Many social evils too have taken ground due to such discrimination. Some evils prevalent widely are female infanticide, female feticide, dowry, sexual harassment, sati, domestic violence, etc.

Whenever there arises any threat to the society, the law comes to the forefront to address the need for curbing the menace of the threat. This process ensures safeguarding the interests and rights of the people. As the evils like female infanticide, female feticide, dowry, sexual harassment, sati, domestic violence, etc. increased the need to curb these arose and to meet this need the laws were enacted to bring gender neutrality in the society.

The gender neutral laws were enacted to prevent the discrimination faced by the women by the discriminating role of the gender. The concept of gender equality has been attempted to be promoted by the gender neutral laws. The biological difference of the two genders has no role to play to be a ground for discrimination between the two in social, economic and political arenas. The gender equality movement aimed at not only preventing discrimination of all kinds but also aim at promoting equal distribution of power, status and property to women.

Female rights activists took up the cause of the women of the country and these efforts led to the enactment of pro-women laws in the country to eradicate the discrimination faced by women. These legislations emancipated women and gave them the recourse to protection.

In the process of setting women free from the shackles of oppression and exploitation the concept of gender neutrality was born. The legislations were enacted keeping in view the alarming rate of increase of the crimes against women and in the backdrop the crimes against men were overshadowed. The laws addressed the concern of the women and at the same time overlooked the concern of the men by assuming that the victims of such crime can only be women. The laws enacted are gender-specific and consider only victimization of women, neglecting the victimization of the opposite gender.

Male- domination and discrimination against women existed on a very large scale in the times which are long gone; today such domination does not exist to that level. With the progress in society the age-old customs and beliefs have been shed too. The laws enacted to protect women against such discrimination serve their purpose to an extent but at the same time neglect the protection of men against such crimes. The laws do not protect men against similar offences and thus puts a question on the equal protection under law which is a fundamental right of every citizen.

The idea of gender-neutrality encompasses the concept of placing both the genders at par, not distinguishing their roles and treating them equally in all spheres. The pro-women laws enacted to curb the discrimination against women has led to discrimination against men, since it has led to no recourse for men in case of their victimization for similar offences.

Both women and men are equally prone to offences like sexual harassment at workplace, sexual assault, domestic violence, rape, etc. When such crimes are committed against both the genders then laws should encompass provisions for the equal protection of both men and women. The laws should not be gender specific and should be made gender neutral. The legislators have so far been under pressure from feminist groups and female rights activists against enacting gender neutral laws over such offences and this is one of the prominent reasons that these laws consider only female victimization.

The laws today are being misused to a great extent, leaving men vulnerable against the stringent provisions of these laws. The people still continue to hold the false beliefs of male superiority and notions about masculinity which makes it an impossible proposition that men can be victims to such offences. Until these notions are shed by the people there cannot be acceptance for the gender neutral laws. The men do not even come forward to report against such offences because of the social stigma they would go through on reporting such offences.

Most of the prominent gender-specific laws were enacted after the Delhi rape case of 2012 which shook the entire nation. The criminal law amendment act

2013[5] brought about more stringent provisions for sexual offences and specific provisions for voyeurism, stalking, sexual harassment etc. Sadly these provisions provide protection to only women and assume perpetrators to be men.

The gender specific laws relating to sexual assault, sexual harassment, dowry death, rape, domestic violence, stalking, voyeurism, etc penalize only men. All these laws assume the perpetrator to be men and victim to be women, there is no room for any provision which would provide protection to men. The legislations urgently need to undergo change in which both men and women are victims and perpetrators. Instead of using words like "men" for perpetrator and "women" for victim, the word "person" needs to be used for both cases.

---

[5]https://www.prsindia.org/sites/default/files/Crimin al%20Law%20%28A%29%20Act%202013.pdf

PATRIARCHY

The subordination of women by men is not just prevalent in India but across many other nations of the world. When we talk in the Indian context then one word strikes hard in the mind of almost everyone and that is 'patriarchy'. We all know that the root cause behind subordination of women in India can be attributed to being the patriarchal set-up of the society.

Women have been subjected to discrimination, humiliation, subjection to cruelty, torture, and exploitation etc over years. The basis of such discrimination not being their sex but gender. As already discussed how gender roles have been assigned to both men and women and how it led to discrimination between the two. Gender is a social construction, based on the roles assigned to different sex.

Patriarchy literally means male dominance. The notion that men are superior to women is the basis of such dominance in the society and family. Men dominate, exploit and control women in all respects. Patriarchy has changed in form overtime but has always remained intact in the societal set-up. It has undergone variations according to time but has not lost its essence of superiority of male over female.

The subordination of women varies in different communities and different places according to the customs followed by them. Patriarchal societies especially Indian patriarchal society believes in the role of women being confined to household chores and rearing of children. Basically their lives hold no meaning except that they have to serve their families especially males. The distinctions of all kinds – social, economic, political which the society imposes are all based on the biological distinction of sex.

The traditional view holds the opinion that it is the biological differences between men and women which have led to different social roles assigned to them. The biological characteristics are believed to determine the roles and capacities. The role of women has been confined to the four walls of the household and even in the household they have always been made to act on the command of the male members.

Today women empowerment is an important social issue which is being addressed nationally and internationally. The need of women empowerment arose from the very subjugation of women. This subjugation has been the result of the suppression of women in all arenas be it social, economic or political owing to patriarchal set-up. The males hold authority over everything- property, family decisions, children, management of societal affairs etc

STRUCTURE IN PATRIARCHY

The family in a patriarchal society is always headed by the male member of the family. The decisions of the head of the family are binding and final and women have no say in the decision making.

In a patriarchal system the birth of a male child is celebrated while the birth of the female child is lamented over. The entire family grieves at the birth of a female as she is considered a liability whereas the male is considered an asset. This preference in the birth of male child has been responsible for evils like female feticide and female infanticide.

This very preference leads to discrimination between the two genders right from the infancy to childhood and then adulthood. The boys are considered to be the inheritors of the family, the ones who would carry on the name of their family whereas the girls are not thought of as a part of the family in which they are born. They are thought of as a liability to be given away in their marriage.

The patriarchal system has not just led to the subjugation of women but the social evils like female feticide, female infanticide, sati, dowry etc are all the result of this societal set-up. As the role of a woman is defined and dependent on a man right from the birth; at the time of birth and till marriage she acts according to the wishes of the father and after marriage according to the wishes of the husband. She is thought to have no purpose without her husband and that is what led to the practice of sati. Ending her life along with her husband had been thought to be the only ethical way of life for a woman. The women who even lived their lives after the end of their husbands' lives lived a miserable and pathetic life. They lived in ostracization and were denied the life of a common person.

The demand for dowry at the time of marriage is also an evil which is based on the belief of male superiority. The marriage by a male with a female has been thought to be a favor conferred on the female and the female's family is ought to repay such in terms of dowry.

The unit of family always mirrors the structure in the society. When in the family the children right from their birth learns these values of suppression, domination and exploitation of the females then what can the society be expected to be. The stereotypes around masculinity and femininity are developed within both men and women as they observe and are brought up in that atmosphere.

This is where the roles start developing, the boys are taught that their role is to earn for the family and control everything whereas the girls are taught that they have to look after the family, take care of children and other members. The acceptance for such roles is due to the fact that their young minds are fed with the fact that this is how the society operates.

The women are not allowed to take part in any political, social or economic areas. And what can we otherwise even expect when they are not even allowed to take decisions for their own life, sexuality, mobility.

This structure perpetuates the ideals of patriarchy as these are passed down from generation to generation.

PATRIARCHY AND RELIGION

In the ancient India women were more or less treated at par with men and their situation worsened during the medieval period.

The patriarchal system has been legitimized by religion. The husband is to be worshipped as god by the wife. The religious institutions legitimized that women should never be made independent and therefore all the powers be vested in men so that women are always dependent on them in either way.

Most of the religions promote patriarchal values. The laws governing marriage, family, divorce, succession, inheritance and adoption are regulated by the religious institutions. Thus all these are under the shadow of the patriarchal beliefs and values.

All the constraints which have been imposed upon women have been designed to keep them subjugated, to prevent their empowerment in any ways possible. They are not allowed to seek education, step outside the domestic space, be in veil before any stranger etc. all the constraints are only for women as these have been designed by men to serve the purpose of men.

Women's Movement

With the grave oppression of women in the society, independent women rights movement started gaining ground which became the voice of the oppressed women. The different movements for women's rights cannot be traced back in some definite chronological order. There have been different developments over time as a result of the movements.

The 19th century witnessed many social reforms to alleviate the suffering of women. The British government too criticized the customs of sati, child marriage, purdah, polygamy etc and considered such customs barbaric. Raja Rammohan Roy, Henry Vivian Derozio, Debendranath Tagore, Keshab Chandra Sen, Ishwar Chand Vidyasagar, Sri Ramakrishna Paramhansa, Swami Vivekanand, Dayanand Saraswati are a few eminent activists who took up the social reform movement in India in the 19th century and with it the cause of the women.

The present day feminists stand for the rights of the women across the world. The term and concept originally from the west takes a strong stand against exploitation and oppression of women and demands equal rights and treatment to women. The movements for women's rights in India are accused to be inspired by western concept and this accusation is based upon the patriarchal bias against the movement demanding any rights for women.

The Indian-ness of the movements which demands equality to women and treatment at par with men is questioned despite India being a nation which strongly upholds the principles of equality. The constitution and the preamble to the constitution also expressly state the concept of equality which the state endeavors to achieve.

The initiation of the movement was with the establishment of autonomous organizations in urban areas. The movement did not reach the common masses of the country. A major section of the society considered this to be an attempt to break the traditional family structure in the society.

POST-INDEPENDENCE

With independence and the enactment and adoption of the constitution which guaranteed equality to all irrespective of sex, caste, creed, gender etc the need for any movement for rights of women became redundant. However over time the actual position of women did not change and further with new socio-economic and socio-political problems the condition of the women worsened.

The patriarchal nature of the society never lost its existence, even years after independence. A number of legislative reforms have been introduced which specifically favor and promote women. Under article 14 where the right to equality is granted, article 15 prohibits discrimination of any kind. But article 15(3) provides that nothing in article 15 can prohibit the state from making special provisions for women and children. And so a number of special provisions were enacted to bring the women on an equal footing with men after years of oppression faced by them.

Not just legislations which deal with women specially but also reservation of seats for women has been provided to enable them to free themselves from the shackles of suppression by providing them the opportunity to participate equally.

Women already went through oppression in all ways possible over years; they were denied education, proper food, employment and were completely made dependent. Along with all these problems in the background new problems arose with the advancement of society.

The exploitation of women began taking new forms like indecent representation of women, sexual harassment at workplace, stalking, voyeurism, gang rape, acid attacks, trafficking for sexual exploitation, etc. So with the traditional problems of female feticide, female infanticide, traditional discrimination against them, dowry demands, dowry deaths, cruelty etc these offences were further added to the list which was to be combated.

Then the need arose for laws addressing the issues of dowry, immoral trafficking, sexual harassment at workplace, etc which paved the way for gender specific legislations which granted protection to women against such offences.

India witnessed heinous offences in the recent past years which received worldwide condemnation. The delhi gang rape case, the mathura rape case, the unnao rape case to mention a few after which very stringent provisions were enacted to deter the commission of such offences.

The gravity and inhumanity of offences especially against women had been observed in the past years and that is what has prompted movements demanding protection to women. India is considered to be one of the most unsafe nation in the world for women. Though we have seen positive advancements in the status of women as compared to the pre-independence period but that advancement has also been restricted to urban areas primarily.

The rural India still continues with practices of veil system, dowry demands, discrimination against women etc. The patriarchal values are upheld by the families in the rural areas. The laws are not abided by the people living in rural areas.

The legislations have achieved their purpose to certain extent but there are factors which still do not change the ground reality.

As the legislature and the judiciary has been vigilant in enacting laws as per the changing needs of the society, these bodies of the government have taken care of the upliftment and protection of women.

With the hue and cry of women's rights in the nation other issues which affect men have receded in the background. All the attention has been diverted to the protection of women's rights. It has been indispensable too but the duty of the law makers is always to anticipate any possible circumstances and formulate laws over it.

The laws like The immoral traffic (prevention) act, 1956, The dowry prohibition act 1961(amended in 1986), The indecent representation of women (prohibition) act 1986, Protection of women from domestic violence act, 2005, The sexual harassment of women at workplace(prevention, prohibition and redressal) act, 2013, The criminal law(amendment) act, 2013,The criminal law amendment act 2018 etc protect the interests of women alone.

It has been assumed due to the overwhelming number of offences against women that only women can fall victim to any such offences and not men. These laws are gender-specific and define the victim and perpetrator on the basis of gender. Only a woman is a victim and a man perpetrator of the offence.

It is such a folly on the part of the society to think that men do not fall prey to any of such offences. In the pursuit of a noble cause of protecting women's rights, the rights of men have been put at stake. They have been denied protection against any such offence and all this is due to the patriarchal nature of the society which has stereotypes surrounding the masculinity of men. The false beliefs of men's superiority and the impossibility of they being victims can all be credited to the patriarchal values.

Where almost all the countries have gender neutral laws with respect to sexual offences, India with the world's second largest population and being the largest democracy in the world has not acknowledged the vulnerability of men to be victims nor does it consider the fact that women can be perpetrators of the offence.

What can this be attributed to? Years of suppression of women at the hands of men, continuous denial of the rights to them, exploitation in every possible means all this has led the people to believe that women have always been vulnerable and continue to be. Therefore the focus always remains on how to bring them in the mainstream and protect their rights.

When any matter comes to the forefront then all the heed is paid to it and when it continues for years then the tendency to hold such assumptions is natural. However there is an urgent need to recognize the fact that the right of men is being taken away by denial for protection to them.

For instance, the Indian Penal Code defines rape as an offence which is committed against a woman by a man. Is it that a man cannot be sexually assaulted by another man or a woman? or can a woman not be assaulted by another woman? As said earlier the duty of the legislature is to take into consideration all the possibilities and here it is not just a possibility but offences which do actually happen. As these are not even defined in the provisions there is no record of the same. These go unreported almost all of the time.

The National Crime Records Bureau would not provide us with the statistics on whether such offences are committed as it takes into account only those which are defined under the law. But that does not mean that those offences do not take place. These are unreported due to two major reasons. First, the stereotypes and taboos that surround masculinity which prevent the victim from approaching for help and second, the unwillingness of the society as a whole to accept the fact that a man can be a victim.

There is no distinction as to the gender of the person in majority of the developed nations when it comes to gender neutrality relating to such laws. The victim or the perpetrator is defined in terms of the word 'person' unlike in India as 'men' and 'women'. Such approach is very much needed in India too.

The women's rights movements and the concept of gender equality fighting against the shackles imposed by patriarchy have attempted to benefit women but the recent developments in the crime against women has brought about a collateral damage to the rights of men. If gender neutrality is propagated then it should serve to the advantage of both the genders and not to the disadvantage of any one.

The patriarchal system of the society has contributed enough to the problems for women and now it is the same beliefs which are hindering the rights of men. Since it is these values only which are denying the very acceptance of the fact that even men are victims and need protection under law like women do.

CONSTITUTIONAL PROVISIONS FOR GENDER NEUTRALITY

1. Article 14 – Equality before law for women

The first and the foremost right which is guaranteed to all the persons is the right to equality. Equality forbids inequalities, unfairness and arbitrariness.

Article 14 provides equality before law - The state shall not deny to any person equality before the law or the equal protection of the laws within the territory of India. Article 14 uses two expressions, "equality before the law" and "equal protection of the laws". The underline principle of Article 14 is that, all persons and things similarly circumstanced should be treated alike, both in privileges conferred and liabilities imposed. Amongst equals, the law should be equal and should be equally administered. In the case

Sanaboina Satyanarayna v. Government of Andhra Pradesh[6] , they formulated a scheme for prevention of crime against women. In prisons also prisoners were classified into two categories, first prisoners guilty of crime against women and second prisoners who are not guilty of crime against women. Prisoners who are guilty of crime against women challenge the court saying that their right to equality is deprived. The court held that classification to keep away prisoners for crimes against women from the benefits of remission, was reasonable, proper and not violative of Article 14.

In **Air India v. Nargesh Meerza**[7], the Supreme Court struck down the Air India and India Airlines regulations on retirement and pregnancy during the services as air hostesses, as unconstitutional. These rules were held

---

[6] CASE NO.: Appeal (crl.) 1227 of 2002
[7] 1981 AIR 1829

to be unreasonable, arbitrary and therefore, violative of Article 14 of the constitution.

2. Article 15 – Prohibition of discrimination on grounds of religion, race, caste, sex or place of birth.

Article 15(1) – Article15 (1) says that 'the state shall not discriminate against any citizen on grounds only of religion, race, caste, sex, place of birth or any of them'.

Article 15(1) is in absolute terms. The grounds of discrimination which are prohibited are religion-race, caste, sex or place of birth. In the case **Raj Rajeshwari Devi v. State of U.P**[8], the U.P. Court of Wards Act, 1912 was challenged. Under this act, while male proprietor could be declared incapable of managing his property only on one of the five grounds mentioned therein and that too after giving him an opportunity

---

[8] AIR 1954 All 608

of showing cause as to why such a declaration should not be meet, a female proprietor could be declared incapable to manage her property on any ground, without giving any her show-cause notice. The provision was held by the court to be bad in law as it amounts to discrimination on the basis of sex.

Article 15(3) – Article 15(3) says that 'nothing in this article shall prevent the state from making any special provision for women and children'.

As per Article 15(1), discrimination on the ground of sex is prohibited, but Article 15(3) allows the state to make special provisions for women and children. To elucidate on the provisions of criminal law, as per section 497 IPC, the offense of adultery can be committed only by a male and not by a female who cannot even be punished as an abettor.

3. Article 16 - Equality of opportunity in matters of public employment

Article 16(1) – Article 16(1) says, 'there shall be equality of opportunity to all citizens in matters relating to employment or appointment to any office under the state'.

The main object of Article 16(1) is to create a constitutional right to equality of opportunity in matters of public employment. Equality of opportunity for all under the state means that public employment or appointment to any office under the state means that public employment and appointment to public office shall be on grounds which do not, exclude any citizen or class of citizen.

Article 16(2) – Article 16(2) says, 'no citizen shall on grounds only of religion, race, caste, sex, decent, place of birth, residence or any of them, be ineligible for, or discriminated against in respect of, any employment or office under the state'.

While Article 16(1) gives in general terms, the right to equality of opportunity, Article 16(2) envisages discrimination against the citizen on grounds of religion, race, caste, sex, decent, place of birth and residence. In the case of **C.B. Muthamma v. Union of India**[9], a service rule requiring a female employee to obtain written permission of the government before the solemnisation of her marriage and denial of right to be appointed on the ground that she was a married woman, was held to be discriminatory.

4. Article 39-A Equal justice and free legal aid

It says that the state shall secure that the operation of legal system promotes justice, on a basis of equal opportunity, and shell, in particular, provide free legal

---

[9] 1979 AIR 1868

aid, by suitable legislation or schemes or in any other way, to ensure that opportunities for securing justice are not denied to any citizen by reason of economic and other disabilities. The principles contained in Article 39-A are fundamental and caste a duty on state to secure that the operation of the legal system promotes justice, on the basis of equal opportunities and further mandates to provide free legal aid in anyway by legislation or otherwise, so that justice is not denied to any citizen by reason of economic or other disabilities.

5. Article 42 – Provision for just and humane conditions of work and maternity relief

Article 42 lays down that state shall make provision for securing just and humane conditions of work and maternity relief. In the case **D. Bhuvan Mohan Patnaik v. State of A.P**[10]. The court stated that directed principles of state policy contained in Article 42 of the constitution maybe extended to the living conditions in jail. Giving meaning to Article 42, the court upheld and granted maternity benefit to non-regularised female workers.

6. Article 46 – Promotion of education and economic interests of Scheduled Castes, Scheduled Tribes and other weaker sections.

Article 46 says that the state shall promote with special care the educational and economic interests of weaker sections of people, and in particular, of the Scheduled Castes and the Scheduled Tribes and shall protect them from social injustice and all forms of exploitation.

7. Article 47 – Duty of the state to raise the level of nutrition and the standard of living and to improve the public health

---

[10] 1974 AIR 2092

Article 47 of the constitution says that the state shall regard the raising of the level of nutrition are in the standards of living of its people and the improvement of public health as among its primary duties and, in particular, the state shall endeavour to bring about prohibition of the consumption, except for medicinal purposes of intoxicating drinks and of drugs which are injurious to health.

8. Article 51-A – Fundamental duties

It shall be the duty of every citizen of India –

(e) to promote harmony and the spirit of common brotherhood amongst all the people of India transcending religious, linguistic and regional or sectional diversities; to renounce practices derogatory to the dignity of the women.

9. Article 238-D – Reservation of seats in panchayat

It states –

(3) not less than one-third (including the no. of seats reserved for women belonging to the Scheduled Castes and Tribes) of the total no. of seats to be filled by direct election in every panchayat shall be reserved for women and such seats maybe allotted by rotation to different constituencies in a panchayat.

(4) not less than one-third of the total no. of offices of chairpersons in the panchayats at each level to be reserved for women.

10. Article 243-T – Reservation of seats

It states –

(3) not less than one-third (including the no. of seats reserved for women belonging to the Scheduled Castes and the Scheduled Tribes) of the total no. of

seats to be filled by direct election in every municipality shall be reserved for women and such seats maybe allotted by rotation to different constituencies in a municipality.

(4) the offices of chairpersons in the municipalities shall be reserved for the Scheduled Castes and the Scheduled Tribes and women in such manner as the legislature of a state may, by law, provide.

INDIAN LAWS

The Indian constitution provides justice, liberty and equality to all its citizens, without discrimination of any kind. The laws legislated by the legislature are in accordance with these principles prescribed by the law of the land i.e., the Indian Constitution. There are however some laws which are gender specific, these define the perpetrator and the victim of the offence to belong to a particular gender.

In India due to the patriarchal background of the society and the continued oppression of the women in the society has led to certain assumptions, that women are always the victims in the hands of men. Though numerically the crime which is committed against women is high as compared to men but not taking notice of the similar crimes committed against men cannot be said to upholding the notion of equality.

There are some women specific legislations where the sole victims are women and the perpetrators are men. In case similar offence is committed against a man, he does not have recourse to protection under law. Some of these legislations which will be discussed in detail are

The Immoral traffic (prevention) act, 1956[11]

The Dowry prohibition act 1961(amended in 1986)[12]

The Indecent representation of women (prohibition) act 1986[13]

Protection of women from domestic violence act, 2005[14]

The Sexual harassment of women at workplace (prevention, prohibition and redressal) act, 2013[15]

---

[11]https://indiacode.nic.in/bitstream/123456789/1661/1/1956104.pdf
[12]http://www.cyberabadpolice.gov.in/information/PDF/acts-laws/act-dowry.pdf
[13] http://legislative.gov.in/sites/default/files/A1986-60_0.pdf
[14]http://chdslsa.gov.in/right_menu/act/pdf/domviolence.pdf
[15] http://www.iitbbs.ac.in/notice/sexual-

Human trafficking is the trade of humans, it comprises of a number of crimes like abduction, kidnapping, illegal confinement, detainment, hurt, grievous hurt, sexual assault, rape, unnatural offences, extraction of organs or tissues, etc. trafficking involves grave human right violations of the humans trafficked. The purpose behind trafficking is forced labour, sexual slavery, commercial sexual exploitation. Human trafficking can occur within a country as well as trans-nationally, it is one of the fastest-growing activities of trans- national criminal organizations.

The trafficked humans are exploited in countless ways with deprivation of all their basic human rights. It is condemned internationally by international agencies and covenants. The recent instruments of international law in preventing human trafficking are the United Nations Protocol to Prevent,

---

Suppress, and Punish Trafficking in Persons, Especially Women and Children, and the United Nations Protocol against the smuggling of Migrants by Land, Sea and Air. The United Nations Office on Drugs and Crime(UNODC) created these conventions and established the United Nations Global Initiative to fight Human Trafficking(UN.GIFT) in 2007[16].

Apart from the above two conventions which specifically deal with the growing menace of human trafficking there are other international instruments which deal with it. The Universal Declaration of Human Rights 1948[17], the International Covenant on Civil and Political Rights 1966[18] and the International Covenant On Economic, Social And Cultural Rights 1966, United Nations convention for the suppression of the traffic in

---

[16] https://www.unodc.org/lpo-brazil/en/trafico-de-pessoas/ungift.html
[17] https://www.un.org/en/universal-declaration-human-rights/
[18]https://www.ohchr.org/en/professionalinterest/pages/ccpr.aspx

persons and of the exploitation of the prostitution of other(1949), and the convention on the elimination of all forms of discrimination against women(1979).

Trafficking in Human Beings is prohibited under the Article 23[19] of the Indian Constitution. Article 23(1) states, "Traffic in human beings and beggar and other similar forms of forced labour are prohibited and any contravention of this provision shall be an offence punishable in accordance with law".

The constitution of India has prohibited trafficking in any form under Part III, which deals with the fundamental rights. These rights are enforceable against the state under Article 32(remedies for enforcement of rights) and Article 226 [20](

---

[19]http://www.legislative.gov.in/sites/default/files/COI-updated-as-31072018.pdf
[20]http://www.legislative.gov.in/sites/default/files/COI-updated-as-31072018.pdf

power of high courts to issue certain writs).

Then there are legislations which deal with the trafficking in human beings. The Protection of Children from Sexual Offences (POCSO) act, 2012, which principally deals with the protection of children from sexual abuse and exploitation. The Immoral traffic (prevention) act 1956 which deals with prevention of trafficking for commercial sexual exploitation. The criminal law (amendment) Act 2013 which substituted section 370 with section 370 and 370A of Indian Penal Code.

The immoral traffic (prevention) act, 1986 was originally the suppression of immoral traffic in women and girls (SITA), 1956 to deal with trafficking in India. However the act only addresses the commercial sexual exploitation or prostitution and the abettors or facilitators of prostitution. The only specific legislation to deal with trafficking actually deals with commercial sexual exploitation of women.

The provisions of the act provide for punishments for keeping a brothel, or allowing premises to be used as a brothel, living on the earnings of prostitution, procuring, inducing or taking person to for the sake of prostitution, seducing or soliciting for purpose of prostitution, etc

All of which revolve around the sexual exploitation of women.

Not going into the details of whether this objective has been met as there are many loopholes in the legislation which hinder the achievement of this objective, the question that comes to the forefront is that despite being named as the 'immoral traffic prevention' act , the act does not address the issue of trafficking in persons (both men and women). The issue at hand which is trafficking has not been actually given due consideration and especially trafficking in men has been neglected almost completely. Why has it not been gender neutral? Has the fact been forgotten that even men are trafficked and exploited in all ways as much as women are.

The trafficking of human beings is so grave that it infringes all the human rights of the trafficked persons, yet the government has provided only a law which protects women and not men. The other legislations also protect children and women from trafficking. The fact that men are also vulnerable to the crime is neglected. Article 23 which abolishes trafficking in human beings does not draw any distinction on the basis of gender then why the legislators overlook the cause of men while enacting laws combating trafficking?

The most important international instrument to combat trafficking in persons is the Protocol to Prevent, Suppress and Punish Trafficking In Persons. India signed the protocol in 2002 and ratified in 2011 which was later codified through some provisions of the criminal law amendment act 2013. There are provisions under the Indian penal code which deal with the various aspects of human trafficking like section 363 A, 366A, 366B, 370 and 370A.

The government has not met the minimum standards required to eliminate trafficking. India is a source, destination and transit country for men, women and children who are subjected to forced labour and sex trafficking. As far as the specific legislation meant to combat the evil of trafficking is concerned the law has not been gender neutral and has overlooked the threat to men by trafficking.

The dowry prohibition act 1961(amended in 1986)

The dowry prohibition act enacted with the aim to prohibit the giving and taking of dowry, dowry which is a social evil that has been prevalent in the Indian society where the bride's parents give exorbitant money, goods or anything in kind at the time of marriage. The dowry system has made the holy institution of marriage as a deal and a means to torment the bride and her family, this has additionally led to an increase in the evils like female feticide and sex discrimination as females are then considered a liability on the family.

With the passing of the dowry prohibition act 1961 the system of dowry was made punishable with both imprisonment and fine. It made dowry a cognizable, non-compoundable and non-bailable offence. The husband and the in-laws are presumed to be guilty unless proved innocent. The purpose behind the insertion of this provision was to safeguard the life and dignity of the women but along with serving this purpose it has been widely misused against the husband and his family. There are incidents where the accused are arrested without any investigation based on a false complaint of dowry harassment.

The provision has been undoubtedly misused in a number of cases. Though this crime has been believed to be gender specific but the provisions have left the men vulnerable at the hands of their wives. The Indian criminal system presumes the innocence of the accused until the guilt is proved beyond reasonable doubt but in this particular case the guilt is presumed and the burden of proving innocence lies on the accused. Moreover the possibility of a similar occurrence in the case of men has been neglected to be considered; the groom and his family can also be harassed for the demand of wealth or kind in consideration for marriage. Though this possibility is far from reality as Indian society has been a male dominant patriarchal society but still there can be cases when such incidents take place. The patriarchal society does not believe in the victimization of men. For such incidents the legislature has nothing to address the issue with, for they do not believe anything of that sort to take place. Is it though not the duty of the legislature to consider every possibility while enacting laws?

The issue of demanding wealth on the pretext of marriage should be addressed as being applicable to both the bride and the groom. There should be neutrality in dealing with the evil. The groom's family has absolutely no recourse to seek protection in case he is harassed for such demands.

Protection of women from domestic violence act, 2005

Domestic violence remains one of the most prevalent forms of violence in the country, though invisible but it accounts for a substantial portion of violence in households.

The act seeks to protect the women form any form of abuse or violence, whether physical, sexual, verbal, emotional and economic which harms the mental or physical well being of the women.

The "aggrieved person" according to section 2(a) of the act, " means a woman who is, or has been, in a domestic relationship with the respondent and who alleges to have been subjected to any act of domestic violence by the respondent". Any woman who resides in the household, which covers not just wife but mother, daughter, sister, child, or any women relative can be an aggrieved person and file a complaint of any violence against her.

Section 3 of the act deals with the definition of domestic violence "For the purposes of this Act, any act, omission or commission or conduct of the respondent shall constitute domestic violence in case it -

(a) harms or injures or endangers the health, safety, life, limb or well-being, whether mental or physical, of the aggrieved person or tends to do so and includes causing physical abuse, sexual abuse, verbal and emotional abuse and economic abuse; or

(b) harasses, harms, injures or endangers the aggrieved person with a view to coerce her or any other person related to her to meet any unlawful demand for any dowry or other property or valuable security; or

(c) has the effect of threatening the aggrieved person or any person related to her by any conduct mentioned in clause (a) or clause (b); or

(d) otherwise injures or causes harm, whether physical or mental, to the aggrieved person.

Explanation I.-For the purposes of this section,-

(i) "physical abuse" means any act or conduct which is of such a nature as to cause bodily pain, harm, or danger to life, limb, or health or impair the health or development of the aggrieved person and includes assault, criminal intimidation and criminal force;

(ii) "sexual abuse" includes any conduct of a sexual nature that abuses, humiliates, degrades or otherwise violates the dignity of woman;

(iii) "verbal and emotional abuse" includes-

(a) insults, ridicule, humiliation, name calling and insults or ridicule specially with regard to not having a child or a male child; and

(b) repeated threats to cause physical pain to any person in whom the aggrieved person is interested.

(iv) "economic abuse" includes- (a) deprivation of all or any economic or financial resources to which the aggrieved person is entitled under any law or custom whether payable under an order of a court or otherwise or which the aggrieved person requires out of necessity including, but not limited to, household necessities for the aggrieved person and her children, if any, stridhan, property, jointly or separately owned by the aggrieved person, payment of rental related to the shared household and maintenance;

(b) disposal of household effects, any alienation of assets whether movable or immovable, valuables, shares, securities, bonds and the like or other property in which the aggrieved person has an interest or is entitled to use by virtue of the domestic relationship or which may be reasonably required by the aggrieved person or her children or her stridhan or any other property jointly or separately held by the aggrieved person; and

(c) prohibition or restriction to continued access to resources or facilities which the aggrieved person is entitled to use or enjoy by virtue of the domestic relationship including access to the shared household.

Explanation II.-For the purpose of determining whether any act, omission, commission or conduct of the respondent constitutes "domestic violence" under this section, the overall facts and circumstances of the case shall be taken into consideration. "

The very definition of domestic violence has taken into account the threats which a woman can face, domestic violence has been defined gender specifically. The act empowers any woman who has been subjected to any act of domestic by the offender, she can herself file a complaint or anyone on her behalf. The complaint can be filed against any male member who has any domestic relationship with the woman, against the husband and all relatives of the husband whether female or male.

The act though address domestic violence does not provide any protection to the men who face any domestic violence. The aggrieved person has only been presumed to be a woman. It has not been recognized by law and the law makers that men can also be subjected to domestic violence, they have completely overlooked the protection needed by men. Only women have been given protection under the same and again gender neutrality has been relegated. Moreover the female relatives

71

of the husband cannot file a complaint against the wife.

Owing to the patriarchal set up of the society, the mere acceptance of the fact that even men can be subjected to cruelty and violence becomes difficult. Adding to the problem, even if a man faces such violence he opts to remain silent about it because he would then face social stigma regarding his masculinity. The society does not recognize intimate partner violence against men as much as it recognizes it against women. The traditional gender roles in society and the stigma that follows upon acceptance of being a victim to any kind of domestic violence by women has resulted in non-reporting of the offence. Hence the number of reporters of domestic violence has been only women.

A victim and the perpetrator of domestic abuse can be both a man and a woman. The law should not be gender biased and needs to be gender neutral.

Rape laws

The offence of rape in India is gender specific as only a woman can get raped in this country and not a man. Rape has been defined under section 375[21] of the Indian Penal Code. The section reads-

A man is said to commit "rape" if he—

(a) penetrates his penis, to any extent, into the vagina, mouth, urethra or anus of a woman or makes her to do so with him or any other person; or (b) inserts, to any extent, any object or a part of the body, not being the penis, into the vagina, the urethra or anus of a woman or makes her to do so with him or any other person; or (c) manipulates any part of the body of a woman so as to cause penetration into the vagina, urethra, anus or any part of body of such woman or makes her to do so with him or any other person; or (d) applies his mouth to the vagina, anus, urethra of

---

[21]https://indiacode.nic.in/bitstream/123456789/421 9/1/THE-INDIAN-PENAL-CODE-1860.pdf

a woman or makes her to do so with him or any other person,

under the circumstances falling under any of the following 7 descriptions:--

First. —Against her will.

Secondly. —Without her consent.

Thirdly. —With her consent, when her consent has been obtained by putting her or any person in whom she is interested, in fear of death or of hurt.

Fourthly .—With her consent, when the man knows that he is not her husband and that her consent is given because she believes that he is another man to whom she is or believes herself to be lawfully married.

Fifthly .—With her consent when, at the time of giving such consent, by reason of unsoundness of mind or intoxication or the administration by him personally or through another of any stupefying or unwholesome substance, she is unable to understand the nature and consequences of that to which she gives consent.

Sixthly .—With or without her consent, when she is under eighteen years of age.

Seventhly .—When she is unable to communicate consent.

Explanation 1 .—For the purposes of this section, "vagina" shall also include labia majora .

Explanation 2 .—Consent means an unequivocal voluntary agreement when the woman by words, gestures or any form of verbal or non-verbal communication, communicates willingness to participate in the specific sexual act:

Provided that a woman who does not physically resist to the act of penetration shall not by the reason only of that fact, be regarded as consenting to the sexual activity.

Exception 1 .—A medical procedure or intervention shall not constitute rape.

Exception 2 .—Sexual intercourse or sexual acts by a man with his own wife, the wife not being under fifteen years of age, is not rape.

The provision is completely gender-specific, only a woman can be a victim of rape and a male can be the perpetrator of the offence. If a man is raped by a woman or man, or a woman raped by a woman, or a transgender is raped then they have nothing to resort to seek protection because the law provides protection only to a woman raped by a man.

There are significant numbers of cases of men being victim to rape or other sexual violence.

In India and some other parts of the world a number of beliefs or myths exist which have so far prevented gender neutrality with regard to this particular offence. It has been believed that rape can only be committed against a female by a male. The myths which support this case are-

Women are physically weak than men- the male stereotypes depict men as being strong, strong enough to protect themselves as well as their family. With such belief it is considered that a woman forcing herself upon a man is simply impossible. Women have been considered the weaker sex and therefore they have been seen to be the victims in the hands of men.

Arousal implies consent- a male must be aroused if he gets an erection or has an orgasm, which means that they are willing to enjoy the sexual activity. Therefore it is physically impossible for a woman to rape a man. But arousal does not imply consent to the sexual act, males get erection even in traumatic or painful sexual situations, mechanical stimulation is needed for erection. Thus this is also a myth which denies the possibility of a woman being able to rape a man.

Males do not undergo trauma- there is the commonly held disbelief that males do not undergo trauma as much as females undergo after going through such incidents. But males undergo more traumatic experience due to the social stigma and disbelief of their victimization. They too undergo hatred, shame, anger and depression in long-term.

On the basis of these and some more commonly held false beliefs, male victimization in case of rape is considered a taboo in Indian society. Thus men have been deprived of the protection from rape under law.

In the case **Tukaram v. State of Maharashtra**[22] popularly known as Mathura rape case, apex court held that the fear which the clause 'thirdly' speaks of is negative by the circumstances. The court held that the victims failure to appeal to companions and her conduct in meekly following the constable

---

[22] 1979 AIR 185

(accused) and allowing him to have his way to the extent of satisfying his lust amounts to consent for the sexual intercourse.

Mathura, an eighteen year old harijan orphan girl was called to the police station on an abduction report filed by her brother at the police station – Desaui ganj in Maharashtra on 26th March, 1972.When they were about to leave the police station, Mathura was kept back at the police station in the late hours of the night by one of the constables, Ganpath, who was on duty. She was taken to a toilet and raped by Ganpath. Then another constable Tukaram, molested and tried to rape her but being too heavily drunk did not succeed. It was alleged that the two constables, while on duty, had volted the doors of police station from inside and plunged the place into the darkness.

The session judge acquitted the accused, on the grounds of tacit consent, of the charge of rape for sexual intercourse between Ganpath and Mathura at the police station.

On appeal, the Bombay High Court reversed the finding of this session judge and found Ganpath guilty of rape and Tukaram guilty for molesting the woman. The high court rightly distinguished between 'consent' and 'passive submission', and held that mere passive or helpless surrender of the body and its resignation to the other's lust has induced by threats or fear cannot be acquitted with desire or will.

The sexual harassment of women at workplace(prevention, prohibition and redressal) act, 2013

The sexual harassment of women at workplace act was legislated to address the growing problem of harassment faced by the women at their workplace. Prior to this act, there were the Vishakha guidelines promulgated by the Supreme Court in the **Vishaka vs State of Rajasthan**[23]. The act provides protection to women against sexual harassment at workplace and provides a mechanism for the redressal of complaints of sexual harassment.

According to section 2 (n) of the act, "sexual harassment includes any one or more of the following unwelcome acts or behavior (whether directly or by implication) namely-

Physical contact and advances; or

A demand or request for sexual favours; or

Making sexually coloured remarks;

or

Showing pornography;

---

[23] (1997) 6 SCC 241

or

Any other unwelcome physical, verbal or non-verbal conduct of sexual nature;

As the participation and emancipation of women increased and women started being equal partners to men in almost all spheres of work, the cases of them being sexually harassed in the workplace rose. Law is dynamic which keeps changing as per the needs of the society and to address this issue for the first time the Supreme Court laid down certain guidelines called the Vishaka guidelines which dealt with sexual harassment of women at workplace. To deal with the issue effectively the legislators enacted the sexual harassment of women at workplace(prevention, prohibition and redressal) act, 2013.

The act very well takes into account the harassment faced by women and seeks to resolve the issue but does not address the similar problem faced by men. The victimization of men is not thought of when sexual harassment is discussed. The number of female victims is definitely more than the male victims but there are cases and the number has been rising of the male victims.

The male victims are harassed both by males and females. Many do not report any case because they fear being ridiculed by the society which does not even consider the fact that a man may face sexual harassment of any sort. They fear embarrassment, mockery and unacceptability by the society. Sexual harassment is not gender specific and the same should be understood by the legislators. It does not depend on the gender of the person. The sexual harassment of men is rising due to lack of legislation on the subject, while the sexual harassment of women is addressed, that of men remains completely unprotected.

The male employees face harassment by female bosses who are in a position to take advantage of their authority or by their male colleagues. It also consists of female on male rape and male on male rape. When a female is harassed then she has recourse to the protection available by law and moreover as people believe that sexual harassment is limited to females so they do not have to go through additional challenges of disbelief by the society. On the other hand when a male undergoes any form of sexual harassment he firstly has no protection under law and secondly he has to face challenges like the stereotypes surrounding his masculinity. He is ridiculed by the society for asserting the predicament that he has been through.

There is no protection by the Indian laws for the male victims of sexual harassment. The legislation is gender specific; the legislators have failed to provide equality in accessing justice to both the genders. The right to equal protection under law has not been actually provided to men in India. Gender neutrality has been forsaken when it comes to enacting laws and providing protection to men against sexual harassment.

The 'right to equality' is infringed when equal protection under law is not provided to men and women equally. There is a need for the legislators to enact gender neutral laws on the subjects where only women are thought to be the victims.

The Nirbhaya case or the 2012 Delhi gang rape case stirred the nation with widespread public protests throughout nation seeking justice for India's daughter. A 23 old female was brutally beaten and gang-raped in New Delhi, Nation's Capital in a bus while travelling. She later succumbed to her injuries; this incident was widely condemned by the people in India and worldwide. Protests were held seeking protection for women in the Nation, demanding the government to formulate stringent laws for dealing with such offences.

Thus the criminal amendment act was passed which brought about changes in the criminal laws dealing with sexual offences namely the criminal procedure code, the Indian penal code and the Indian evidence act. These changes were brought about by the recommendations of the Justice Verma Committee, which was constituted with the purpose of providing recommendations for amendment.

From the many changes which were brought about by the amendment act, there were some provisions which were completely gender-specific. The victimization of only women is considered in such provisions. The important ones being, section 354A, 354B, 354C, 354D, 376, 376A, 376B, 376C, 376D and 376E of the Indian Penal Code.

'354A. (1) A man committing any of the following acts—

physical contact and advances involving unwelcome and explicit sexual overtures; or

a demand or request for sexual favours; or

showing pornography against the will of a woman; or

making sexually coloured remarks, shall be guilty of the offence of sexual harassment.

(2) Any man who commits the offence specified in clause (i) or clause (ii) or clause (iii) of sub-section (1) shall be punished with rigorous imprisonment for a term which may extend to three years, or with fine, or with both.

(3) Any man who commits the offence specified in clause (iv) of sub-section (1) shall be punished with imprisonment of either description for a term which may extend to one year, or with fine, or with both.

354B. Any man who assaults or uses criminal force to any woman or abets such act with the intention of disrobing or compelling her to be naked in any public place, shall be punished with imprisonment of either description for a term which shall not be less than three years but which may extend to seven years, and shall also be liable to fine.

354C. Any man who watches, or captures the image of a woman engaging in a private act in circumstances where she would usually have the expectation of not being observed either by the perpetrator or by any other person at the behest of the perpetrator or disseminates such image shall be punished on first conviction with imprisonment of either description for a term which shall not be less than one year, but which may extend to three years, and shall also be liable to fine, and be punished on a second or subsequent conviction, with imprisonment of either description for a term which shall not be less than three years, but which may extend to seven years, and shall also be liable to fine.

Explanation 1.—For the purpose of this section, "private act" includes an act of watching carried out in a place which, in the circumstances, would reasonably be expected to provide privacy and where the victim's genitals, posterior or breasts are exposed or covered only in underwear; or the victim is using a lavatory; or the victim is doing a sexual act that is not of a kind ordinarily done in public.

Explanation 2.—Where the victim consents to the capture of the images or any act, but not to their dissemination to third persons and where such image or act is disseminated, such dissemination shall be considered an offence under this section.

354D. (1) Any man who—

follows a woman and contacts, or attempts to contact such woman to foster personal interaction repeatedly despite a clear indication of disinterest by such woman; or

 monitors the use by a woman of the internet, email or any other form of electronic communication; or

 watches or spies on a woman in any manner, that results in a fear of violence or serious alarm or distress in the mind of such woman, or interferes with the mental peace of the woman, commits the offence of stalking:

 Provided that such conduct shall not amount to stalking if the man who pursued it proves that— (i) it was pursued for the purpose of preventing or detecting crime and the man accused of stalking had been entrusted with the responsibility of prevention and detection of crime by the State; or (ii) it was pursued under any law or to comply with any condition or requirement imposed by any person under any law; or (iii) in the particular circumstances such conduct was reasonable and justified.

(2) Whoever commits the offence of stalking shall be punished with imprisonment of either description for a term which shall not be less than one year but which may extend to five years, and shall also be liable to fine.'.

Reading through the sections makes it amply clear that all the provisions are gender specific, there is no neutrality with respect to the victim and the perpetrator of the crime. The perpetrator is assumed to be a man and the victim a woman. It is assumed that only men can commit such offences and women are the sole victims of such offences, and based on such assumptions only the law has been formulated, providing protection only to women and punishment to men.

Men have no recourse to any type of such sexual offences, they face social stigma and are traumatized more than women. There is no legal redress made available to them by the government, and when the government itself assumes that the offence cannot be committed against men then the assumption of the society is more than obvious. These victims undergo trauma for the rest of their lives, having to even remain silent of all that they go through. They cannot even seek justice for themselves, they become mute victims of sexual offences. The law fails to provide protection to them for such offences where the perpetrator and the victim cannot be gender defined. The wrong assumptions and myths of male masculinity make them suffer at the hands of offenders.

The Indecent Representation of Women (prohibition) act 1986

An act of 1986 passed to prohibit any form of indecent representation of women in any publications, advertisements, writings, paintings, figures or in any other manner. The act seeks to protect the honor of the women by criminalizing any publication of the depiction of women in an indecent manner.

Section 2(c) of the act defines indecent representation of women as "the depiction of the figure of a woman, her form or body or any part thereof in such a way as to have effect of being indecent, or derogatory to or denigrating, women, or is likely to deprave, corrupt or injure the public morality or morals".

The act has very well taken into account the public morality which needs to be maintained and taken care of in the society. However the law is gender specific and does not provide similar protection to men. If a man or his body or any part thereof is depicted in any way which is indecent or derogatory then he cannot seek protection under the law.

The legislature considers only indecent representation of women to be against public morals and not the representation of men. Is public morality only about women in the society or are women only affected by derogatory or denigrating depiction of their body?

The law should be gender neutral and prohibit the indecent representation of a person and not a specific gender.

Torture, both mental and physical (Section 498-A IPC)[24]

Section 498A – Husband or relative of husband of a woman subjecting her to cruelty – whoever, being the husband or the relative of the husband of the woman, subjects such woman to cruelty shall be punished with imprisonment for a term which may extend to three years and shall also be liable.

For the purpose of this section, "cruelty" means

(a) Any wilful conduct which is of such a nature as is likely to drive the woman to commit suicide or to cause grave injury or danger to life, lymph or health

---

[24]https://httpps://indiacode.nic.in/bitstream/123456789/421
9/1/THE-INDIAN-PENAL-CODE-1860.pdf

(whether mental or physical) of a woman; or

(b) Harassment of the woman where such harassment is with a view to coercing her or any person related to her to meet any unlawful demand for any property or valuable security or is on account of failure by her or any person related to her to meet such demand.

While in **State v. Bijay**[25], the Andhra Pradesh and the Delhi high court judgements upheld that the word 'cruelty' is well defined in section 498A, IPC, the judgement of the Calcutta high court as reported in Indian Express , in a similar situation shows its pitfalls. In this case fifteen year old Rina was married to Bijay after 6 months of alleged cruelty and demands for dowry of Rs. 2000 and tape recorder she committed suicide. Several relatives led evidence to show

---

[25] CASE NO.: Appeal (crl.) 1339-1340 of 1999

that Rina was subjected to cruelty, but the court ruled that the uncorroborated evidence of relatives could not be accepted. There were no physical signs of cruelty. Mental torture by forcing her to do domestic work, after turning out (dismissing) all the servants in the affluent home, was not established. Besides, it is also very much doubtful if doing domestic duties in the absence of servants maybe considered torture, let alone torture enough to make a housewife prefer death to get away from it all, says the judgement.

The girl had told her mother and her aunt that they would not be able to see her unless the demands of the husband were met. But the court could not relate these demand with the suicide as there were only three weeks between the two, and it was two short spans during which cruel treatment was allegedly meted out to Rina. The court also found the girl sentimental and imaginative from her letters. Therefore, the mother in law and the husband, who were charged with abetting her to commit suicide were let off.

Those who know the social situation in which dowry deaths take place will find it difficult to agree with the reasoning of high court. The range of mental cruelty is a vast and intractable terrain, as the Andhra judgement observed, and being forced to do domestic work in the early weeks of marriage after the dismissal of servants would amount to both physical and mental cruelty. If the girl is sentimental and imaginative such treatment is or the more bound to hurt the teenage psych.

This judgment underlines the fact that it is not enough to pass legislation against social events unless it is actively supported by investigating authorities, who can make a full proof case, and a judge whose intellect reflect the social contact in which we live, it is difficult to implement the social welfare laws.

Molestation (Section 354 IPC)

Section 354 – Assault or criminal force to woman with intent to outrage her modesty – whoever assaults or uses criminal force to any woman intending to outrage or knowing it to be likely that he will thereby outrage her modesty, shall be punished with imprisonment of either description for a term which may extend to 2 years, or with fine, or with both.

Section 354, IPC has been enacted with a view to protect a woman against an indecent assault as well as to save that public morality and decent behaviour. The section punishes and assault, or use of criminal force to any woman with the intention or knowledge that the woman's modesty will be outraged.

In the case **Rupan Deol Bajaj**[26], the Supreme Court held that slapping a woman on her posterior amount to 'outraging of her modesty' within section 354 and 509, IPC. At a dinner party on July 18th, 1988 Mr K.P.S Gill, then director general of police, of the state of Punjab came and stood in front of Mrs Bajaj a senior of I.A.S officer so close that his legs were about four inches from her knees. He then asked her 'to get up immediately' and come along with him and on her objection slapped her on the posterior in the full presence of all the guests.

It appears the police did not initiate any action on the first information report of Mrs Bajaj and the high court of Punjab and Haryana allowed the petition of Mr Gill for quashing of F.I.R on the ground that matter being too trivial, it needs no action.

Allowing the petition of Mrs Bajaj, the supreme court held that the alleged act of Mr Gill in slapping Mrs Bajaj on her posterior amounted to 'outraging her

---

[26] 1996 AIR 309

modesty' within section 354 and 509, IPC for it was not only an affront (disrespectful) to the normal sense of feminine decency but also an 'upfront of her dignity'.

Prostitution and Sex Tourism of Boys In India

In various studies it was found that prostitution and sex tourism of male children is rampant in major pilgrimage centers of India. Due to development of tourism without proper and protective measures leads to sexual exploitation of children, in the form of child labor, child prostitution, child trafficking, child abuse. There is a huge rise in the demand of male children for all these purposes. These children are exploited by domestic and foreign tourist as well. Due to extreme poverty and less means of survival, they are forced to prostitution.

Criminal Law Amendment Act 2018

The criminal law amendment act 2018 also emerged as a result of some barbaric incidents which took the nation in shock at the extent to which atrocities can be committed. The Kathua rape case and the Unnao rape case were the two infamous cases which demanded even more stringent laws to deter the perpetration of such heinous offences.

The amendment has made the provisions even more stringent and also introduced the punishment of death penalty for rape cases. It has classified the punishments and the offence of rape as per the age of the victim. There are three categories of punishment for rape –

Rape on a woman under twelve years of age being punishable with a minimum 20 years of imprisonment and maximum life imprisonment or death. In case of gang rape minimum life imprisonment and maximum life imprisonment or death.

Rape on a woman under sixteen years of age punishable with a minimum 20 years of imprisonment and maximum life imprisonment. In case of gang rape minimum life imprisonment.

Rape on a woman of sixteen and above punishable by minimum 10 years and maximum life imprisonment.

There are other changes too in the procedure making the speedy trial and investigation possible and other dealing with the bail application.

The difference between the punishments for rape of a girl or a boy has been widened by the amendment in the IPC. Prior to the amendment the punishment prescribed for the offence against a boy or girl under the POCSO act was the same.

Thus with the amendments and the changes which are being brought about in the laws dealing with sexual offences the gender neutrality concept in laws has been facing a setback. Firstly, the offence of rape against men is not defined in the IPC and then the laws are getting more stringent imposing a threat to the innocent men who are falsely accused of such offences. Secondly, now there is disparity in the punishment in case of rape of minor children, punishment being more in case of offence committed against minor girl.

These incidents which are responsible for a demand in more stringent laws for the protection of women take all the attention to how vulnerable the women in the country are and make us believe that men are always perpetrators. However men too have a right to protection under law for any such offence committed against them. The discrimination is not justifiable on the ground of the commonly held belief that only women are the victims. A victim and a perpetrator can belong to any gender whatsoever and drawing a distinction between the two on the basis of gender is not acceptable.

<u>Domestic Violence</u>

Domestic violence is today's reality in many parts of the world. Generally, domestic violence is seen as a synonymous with violence against women. Women only seen as a victim of domestic violence and men as a perpetrator, but most of the men victims continued to suffer in silence from their partner. The book focuses on the phenomenon of domestic violence against men with the women as perpetrator with a view towards gender balancing. The book shows the need for a law of gender equality.

The literal meaning of the "Domestic Violence" means any violent or aggressive behavior of any person within the home as the word "domestic" dictionary meaning is relating to a running of a home or to family relation. Basically from the ages domestic violence has been committed against women but in today's scenario men can also file for domestic violence which can come under the category of domestic abuse, family violence arising out of relationship such as marriage, family members, family friends, etc. and it can be in various forms such as physical aggressions, sexual abuse, emotional abuses, etc. Domestic violence arises when one intimate partner uses physical force, violence, coercion, threat, intimidation, isolation or emotional, sexual or economic abuse to maintain power and control over the other intimate person. There is no such physical act which characterizes domestic violence but it encompasses behaviors of abusing, false imprisonment, sexual abuse, etc.

This form of violence is very common in India. But more cases of domestic violence is registered against men and women are victim. To prevent these atrocities against women at International and National level many efforts are being made so that these types of crimes can be controlled. The entire focus of domestic violence is on women as it is perceived notion that definitely men will be the perpetrator and women will be victim but the domestic violence against men is also increasing gradually in India. The supremacy of men in the society makes everyone believe that they are not vulnerable to domestic violence.

For centuries, it has been depicted in various mythologies, literature, and forms of expressions that women are inferior and men are superior. Therefore, men are supposed to be powerful, aggressive, and women on the receiving end as oppressed and silent sufferers of all forms of violence. These notions are mostly guided by gender roles and norms where women cannot be violent, aggressive or oppressive because of their social positions. But, it is a known fact that that the power relations, gender roles, norms, and values are not static, and they change over time. It has always been widely assumed that women are always the victims and men the perpetrators. There are many reasons behind this assumptions. The idea that men could be victims of domestic abuse and violence is so unthinkable that many men do not even attempt to report the violence. Acceptance of violence by women on men is generally considered as a threat to men folk, their superiority and masculinity.

Although there is no systematic study or record on domestic violence against men in India, it is generally estimated that in 100 cases of domestic violence, approximately 40 cases involve violence against men. There is little evidence available about the actual number of violent acts against men and underlying dynamics of violence. There are various reasons for under-reporting, but foremost among them are our social system and values attached to men, which stop them from sharing and reporting domestic violence and abuse. Even when men report domestic abuse and violence, most people do not believe them. When men try to narrate their problems, torture, struggle, and harassment within marriage and family, no one listens to them; instead, they are mocked. Many men are ashamed of talking about and sharing that they are beaten by their wives.

Men tolerate and stay in abusive and violent relationship for many reasons. Some of the reasons "why men tolerate domestic violence and abuse" are the belief and hope that things would get better, fear of losing social respect and position, protection, and love toward their children and family. Many abused men feel that they have to make their marriages work. They are afraid that if things fall apart, they will be blamed. Many abused men also believe that it is their fault and feel that they deserve the treatment they receive. Another reason is increasing economic and other dependency on women.

Violence against men is not considered serious because of its different manifestation. In most cases of violence against men, women use more mental, verbal, and emotional violence and abuse and are involved less in physical violence. The impact of violence against men is less apparent and is less likely to come to the attention of others. A significant number of men are over sensitive to emotional and psychological abuse. In some cases, humiliating a man emotionally in front of others can be more devastating than physical abuse. Mental and emotional abuse can be an area where women are often more brutal than men. However, what hurts a man mentally and emotionally can in some cases be very different from what hurts a woman.

For some men, being called a coward, impotent, or a failure can have a very different psychological impact than it would have on a woman. Unkind and cruel words hurt in different ways and linger in different ways. In most cases, men are more deeply affected by emotional abuse than physical abuse. The only way to stop false cases is to work towards rigorous prosecution of all false cases and false evidences, including wrong investigation by police.

Technically speaking there are few laws which are gender neutral . For example IPC 323, IPC 406 , IPC 307 and many more . But if you ask specifically for men there are no laws.

If you are a man and you want to use above laws against your wife, you will find it next to impossible . First of all no police station will register your complaint ,if they register they will not take any action for long time . Everyone has that deep rooted misandry inside which stops them from pointing finger towards women. This misandry never allowed law makers to make any law or even discussion on men. There is a dire need of lot of research and literature on men in India .

Well, there are none. India feminists have taken over law making and judiciary completely. As per the feminists:

Domestic violence: Minister of women child decelopment Ms. Maneka gandhi says "all violence is male generated". Having such a sexist and discriminatory thought process is self explanatory as to why there are no laws for Men who are facing violence from their partners.

Rape: **Indian society laughs on a man of he says he has been raped**. India ridicules any complaint of male rape. Indian feminists and society thinks that only Men are preperators of a henious crime like rape and women can rape a man. Owing to such psyche there are no laws for men who are survivors of rape.

Narendra v K.Meena (Civil appeal no. 3253 of 2008, decided on 2016)

The Supreme Court of India had decided that the coercion or forcing the husband to leave his parents (who are dependent on his income) amounts to cruelty on part of the wife, therefore can be a strong ground for divorce under Hindu Law.

Raj Talreja v. Kavita Talreja[27]

In this case, there were false allegations made by the wife against the husband. The court held that this amounts to mental cruelty and can be a ground for divorce.

Well, there are none. India feminists have taken over law making and judiciary completely. As per the feminists:

If law can favour women, then there will be no need to conduct any trial or ask parties to submit their evidences, conduct cross-examinations, indulge in useless legal arguments. It will be much simpler to peruse the complaint/FIR and simply pronounce the husband as guilty and punished for 3 years in jail under IPC 498A etc.

---

27 CIVIL APPEAL NO. 10719 OF 2013

One needs to understand that dynamics of domestic violence and abuse among men and women are different, with different reasons, purposes, and motives. There are various studies on dynamics of violence against women, but there are limited studies on the issue of domestic violence and abuse against men.

Domestic violence against men by their spouse and family members has become an important issue in today's generation and became the form of domestic violence under the judiciary. In comparison to violence against women, violence against men in India is less frequent and less reported but it has already taken a drastic shape/change in most of the countries of the world including India.

WHY VIOLENCE AGAINST MEN IS NOT REPORTED?

Most of the cases of domestic violence go unreported so it is difficult to get exact number on domestic violence and it is even more difficult to figure out that how many men are suffering from abuse or domestic violence. The main reason that most of the violence against the men are remain to be unreported is the traditional gender roles in society and the stigma of the perceived weakness to admit or confess of falling victim to a woman.

Although some research suggest that the domestic violence committed by men and women are equal in numbers but the reported victims are mainly female. The reason for the difference in reported victims might be because of the men who call police to report the domestic violence against them fear of police as they might end up being getting arrested.

The second reason for the same could be that the word man is itself a gender-biased which denotes power, full of masculine behavior, appearances and control of emotions. It is a common belief or we can say that a common perception that distinguishes male and female in terms of expression of their feelings. It could be harder as well as a matter of shame for men to disclose their suffering in a male-dominated society. It can be perceived as a "feminine behavior" in the society. This is the reason the men fear to share his feeling to any of his friend or family members and he starts living in distress, loneliness and not able to disclose his feelings to anybody.

The third reason could be the unavailability of proper sources to men for example: proper enactment of law for male as there are for female under IPC and CrPC, counseling services, institutional support, family support, help lines, etc.

As long as the common misconception that men are always the abuser and women are always the victim will remain in the society, the male victims will feel fear and uncomfortable reporting about domestic violence.

DYNAMICS RELATED TO VIOLENCE AGAINST MALES

The word "violence" is generally referred in the terms of cognitive interpretations. It basically relates to power dynamics i.e., who is more powerful male or female? Male violence is the interpretation of power, can be in terms of economic empowerment or the level of insecurities i.e., who feels more insecure of leaving whom.

For example, if a male earns less than a female and his wife starts analyzing the situation and feels more empowered and powerful, and the women starts bashing the male for it than it develops insecurity within the men and can even be a victim of violence thereafter.

This can be seen in professional field also, if the workplace is headed by active, socially strong women in status, physical robustness, mental strength, and psychological power.

There are no absolute principles for understanding the emotional differences between men and women and the dynamics of violence. However, there are principles that provide interpretation of individual situations.

Norm violation theory by De Ridder and Tripathi[28] (1992) is one such principle that can be used to explore violent reactions and the underlying factors. Norm violation theory looks at the cycle of conflict-dynamics and predicts whether it is going to follow the cycle of escalation or de-escalation. The precipitating factor is taken as a norm violation. It is in this context that norm-violation theory can be used to understand how a certain action on the part of the male/female may be seen as malevolent and lead to a violent

---

[28] DeRidder, R. R. & Tripathi, R. C. (1992). Norm violation and intergroup relations. Oxford, UK: Clarendon Press.

(retributive or tit-for-tat) reaction by the partner. Male victims of domestic violence deserve the same recognition, sympathy, support, and services as do female victims. Domestic violence mostly leaves the victim depressed and anxious irrespective of gender. Consequently, male victims should be listened to and cared for. Male victims must be prepared to speak out

their situations because men are traditionally thought to be physically stronger than women, they might be less likely to talk about or report incidents of domestic violence in their heterosexual relationships due to embarrassment or fear. Men should start telling someone about the abuse and not hesitate about the same, whether it's a parents, friend, relative, health care provider or other close contact. At first, it might be difficult due to the male ego, but in the end, it is likely to bring about relief and the much-needed support.

Society is changing with time and so are the values. Men has started facing torture and harassment by women/spouse so the time has come to address their issue and problems as a social issue and develop appropriate strategies and interventions to cure this problem.

They are no longer stronger than women now, but women come at the same footing as the men are. This is the reason they need a help in crisis and violence particularly violence by spouse/wife. Male victims of the domestic violence can be helped through the appropriate intervention such as recognition of violence against men by women; enactment of relevant piece of legislation; helpline for the male victims of violence; and education, awareness, and legal safeguards.

Effective legislations to curb domestic violence against men must be put in place and enforced. Law enforcement agents should accept that domestic violence against men is a reality, from which men should be protected. The brutality of a man by his wife should not be seen as a trivial domestic matter. The trials of women who batter or kill their husbands must be given wide publicity in order to serve as deterrence to others who may have such

tendencies. There should be greater advocacy to enlighten the public about the existence and reality of the evil of domestic violence against men by government agencies, religious groups and civil rights organizations. This will help in balancing the gender discourse on domestic violence and bring about better families in the Indian society. Gender activism must involve a balance of power in relationships in order not to arrogate too much power to the women, who will then turn around to use such power to oppress the men. It is the contention of this book, that as we protect the right of women in the marriages, similarly the rights of men should be protected. Also just like women, men deserve protection from intimate partner brutality and abuse, and also have a right for better living as married men.

Adultery

Adultery, the age old complaint of society, probably is one of the few issues which are dealt frequently in connection with controversies that arise due to rapid changes of mentality of people especially in Indian scenario where conservative perspective is no longer considered as valuable as used to be accepted in the past. Adultery or in other words-"Violation of marriage bed" is an invasion on the right of a husband over his wife, as people think, perhaps reflects the same motive behind the great war of the "Ramayana" that started after· abduction of Sita by Ravana and Sita had to go for 'Agnipariksha' to prove her chastity.

But when we see today's society, we find an absolute change that either has come or just awaiting to influence the moral values of present generation.

A bare reading of Section 497 of the Indian Penal Code, 1860[29] shows that it punishes the offence of adultery committed with a married woman without the consent or connivance of her husband. The main feature of this offence is that the male offender alone has been made liable. This offence is committed by a third person against a husband in respect of his wife. If an act of sexual intercourse takes place between a married man and an unmarried woman or with a widow or with a married woman whose husband consents to it, this offence shall not be deemed to have been committed. It is not required for an offence under this section that the offender should know whose wife the women is, but he must know that she was a married woman.

In **Sowmithri Vishnu v. Union of India[30]** and another(1985) it was contended that section 497, IPC is violative of Articles

---

[29]https://indiacode.nic.in/bitstream/123456789/421 9/1/THE-INDIAN-PENAL-CODE-1860.pdf
[30] 1985 AIR 1618

14 and 15 of the Constitution on the ground that it makes an irrational classification between men and women. It confers upon the husband the right to prosecute the adulterer but it does

not confer any right upon the wife to prosecute the women with whom her husband committed adultery; it does not confer any right on the wife to prosecute the husband who has committed adultery with another woman.; it does not take in cases where the husband has sexual relation with an unmarried woman with the result that it amounts to having a free licence under the law to have extra marital relationship with unmarried woman. However, the Apex Court previously rejected these afore said contentions and held that it cannot be said that in defining the offence of adultery so as to restrict the class of offender to men, any constitutional provision is infringed. It is commonly accepted that it is the man who is seducer and not the women. In this case, the Apex Court observed that this position might have undergone some change over the years that women may have started seducing men but it is for the legislature to take note of this transformation and amend section 497 appropriately. In the aforesaid

case, it was also contended that since section 497 of IPC does not contain provision for hearing wife, therefore, it is violative of Article 21 of the Constitution i.e., freedom of personal liberty.

In connection with this question the Court observed that this section is not violative of Article 21, because although this section does not contain provision for hearing of married women with whom the accused is alleged tovhave committed adultery but if she makes an application in the trial court that she should be given an opportunity of being heard, she would be given that opportunity. Neither substantive nor adjective criminal law prohibits the court from providing a hearing to a party, which is likely to be adversely affected by the decision of the Court directly or indirectly.

As per the patriarchal mindset of our society woman has no entity and she is a non-person

An analysis of Section 497 of IPC along with the various observations by the Supreme Court of India and High Courts, bring us to the conclusion that only a man can commit adultery. The married woman who is involved in the conduct is not punishable as the adultery. The married woman who is involved in the conduct is not punishable as the adulterer, because she is treated as a "victim", not as "the author of the crime", because she has no entity and she is a non-person. The section negates the free will of the woman in adulterous conduct and does not concern itself with the intentions behind her act. Further, women whose lives are affected by the crime of adultery the aggrieved wives if the adulterer is married are not deemed to be necessary and interested parties in the

125

trial or in its criminal consequences. This is because the woman is looked upon as an object, an inanimate property, whose rights are almost transferable. Property on its own has no legal existence. Moreover, if a married man has sexual intercourse with an unmarried woman it is no adultery because an unmarried woman does not belong to anybody as property and is not owned by anybody, not even her parents or brother because they hold her in trust and have no ownership rights to prosecute the person.

The makers of the law seemed to have thought that the sanctity of matrimonial home would be violated if either of the parties resorts to adultery. The law is thus blatantly biased against the woman. It has put the man in a privileged position by treating the relationship between husband and wife as one of the owner and owned. The section is only meant to punish the adulterer because he has laid his hands on another man's property i.e., wife and tried to steal the same. The law continues to treat woman as a nonperson and an object, giving her the status of property. The idea of equal status, identity and liberty should be fundamental to any democratic civilization. A law, which forces the woman to live under a code imposed by man, totally negating the feminine viewpoint, is alien to truly humanistic values.

THE SUPREME COURT STRUCK DOWN SECTION 497 OF THE INDIAN PENAL CODE AND DECRIMINALISED ADULTERY IN INDIA: AN ANALYSIS WITH SPECIAL REFERENCE TO

JOSEPH SHINE V. UNION OF INDIA (2017)[31]

Five-judge bench of the Supreme Court struck down Section 497 of the Indian Penal Code in Joseph Shine v. Union of India (2017) and decriminalized adultery in India, however adultery remains a

---

[31] WRIT PETITION (CRIMINAL) NO. 194 OF 2017

civil offence. Adultery can be a ground for divorce. The judgment directly blows the archaic and patriarchal law in our country. This judgment is also important because of its consequences for the future.

A husband is not the master and equality is the governing parameter Supreme Court in Joseph Shine v. Union of India (2017) has clearly laid down that the beauty of the Indian Constitution is that it includes I, you and we. The Court further asserted that *"Such a magnificent, compassionate and monumental document embodies emphatic inclusiveness, which has been further nurtured by judicial sensitivity when it has developed the concept of golden triangle of fundamental rights. In such a situation, the essentiality of the rights of women gets the real requisite space in the living room of individual dignity rather than the space in an annex to the main building. That is the manifestation of concerned sensitivity. Individual dignity has a sanctified realm in a civilized society. The civility of a civilization earns warmth and respect when it respects more the individuality of a woman. The said concept gets a further accent when a woman is treated*

with the real spirit of equality with a man. Any system treating a woman with indignity, inequity and inequality or discrimination invites the wrath of the Constitution. Any provision that might have, few decades back, got the stamp of serene approval may have to meet its epitaph with the efflux of time and growing constitutional precepts and progressive perception. A woman cannot be asked to think as a man or as how the society desires. Such a thought is abominable, for it slaughters her core identity. In addition, it is time to say that a husband is not the master. Equality is the governing parameter. All historical perceptions should evaporate and their obituaries be written."

In Joseph Shine v. Union of India, (2017) ,the Supreme Court asserted that the binding nature of precedent should not be allowed in order to retain the status of precedent or allowed to be diluted. The

Court observed that "When a constitutional court faces such a challenge, namely, to be detained by a precedent or to grow out of the same because of the normative changes that have occurred in the other arenas of law and the obtaining precedent does not cohesively fit into the same, the concept of cohesive adjustment has to be in accord with the growing legal interpretation and the analysis has to be different, more so, where the emerging concept recognizes a particular right to be planted in the compartment of a fundamental right, such as Articles 14 and 21 of the Constitution. In such a backdrop, when the constitutionality of a provision is assailed, the Court is compelled to have a keen scrutiny of the provision in the context of developed and progressive interpretation. A constitutional court cannot remain entrenched in a precedent, for the controversy relates to the lives of human beings who transcendentally grow. It can be announced with certitude that transformative constitutionalism asserts itself every moment and asserts

itself to have its space. It is abhorrent to any kind of regressive approach."

In the above –mentioned judgment the Apex Court clearly laid down that there is need to adopt transformative constitutionalism.

The women cannot be considered as a property of men in the modern progressive jurisprudential parameters and expansive constitutional vision.

In the relationship between a husband and wife, it is improbable to allow a criminal offence to enter and make a third party culpable.

The Supreme Court has declared 150 years old law on adultery as unconstitutional, which treats a husband as the master. The then Chief Justice of India declares, "The adultery law is arbitrary and it offends the dignity of a woman," In this recent landmark judgment, the Apex Court directly blows the archaic and patriarchal law in our country. Supreme Court in Joseph Shine v. Union of India(2017) has clearly laid down that the beauty of the Indian Constitution is that it includes I, you and we. Court asserted that the binding nature of precedent should not be allowed in order to retain the status of precedent or allowed to be diluted. The women cannot be considered as a property of men in the modern progressive jurisprudential parameters and expansive constitutional vision. The provisions as contained under section 497 of IPC indicate that women are treated as subordinate to men.

It further lays down that when there is consent of the man to develop relationship outside the wedlock then there is no offence. The Court declares that husband is not the master of wife. Section 497 of IPC is absolutely and manifestly arbitrary and irrational because it confers a license on the husband to deal with the wife, as he likes which is extremely excessive and disproportionate. The Apex court declare that autonomy, desire, choice and identity are the important aspects of the dignity of a woman.

In this regard, the Apex Court refers the recent judgment K.S. Puttaswamy and another v. Union of India and others (2017) in which court declares that right to privacy is a fundamental right as prescribed under Article 21 of the Constitution. The Court has recognized the conceptual equality and dignity of woman, which cannot be curtailed. However, Section 497 of IPC curtails the dignity and equality of women because it is based on gender stereotypes and these types of stereotypes put a serious blow on the individual's dignity of women. the Apex Court declares that there cannot be a patriarchal monarchy over the daughter as well as husband's monarchy over the wife. Male dominance is unacceptable in today's scenario. Moreover the Supreme Court in asserted that adultery can be ground for civil issues such as dissolution of marriage however, it cannot be a criminal offence. In case of adultery, criminal law expects people to be loyal which is a command however this command gets into the realm of privacy.

Adultery might not be the cause of an unhappy marriage however; it could be the result of an unhappy marriage.

Along with Section 497 of IPC, section 198 of CrPC is also declared unconstitutional thereby decriminalizing the offence of adultery. Justice D.Y. Chandrachud asserted that "the history of Section 497 reveals that the law on adultery was for the benefit of the husband, for him to secure ownership over the sexuality of his wife. It was aimed at preventing the woman from exercising her sexual agency."

However, the judgment has a variety of impacts on the institution of marriage in India from which some are positive and some are negative which cannot be ignored. Decriminalization of adultery would badly endanger the institution of marriage in India. Decriminalization will give license to the married parties to set up an extra marital affair. The divorce cases would increases with such extramarital affairs, which would badly affect the future of their children and institution of marriage.

Stalking

Stalking is a form of harassment comprising of repeated and persistent following with the intention of harming or causing fear to the person being followed. It can be in various forms- physical or online and under the law only a man can stalk a woman. This means that, the law is not gender neutral and the recourse is only for the woman.

If a man follows a woman to contact her or contacts her to foster any interaction, then this amounts to stalking. A woman may or may not know she is being stalked and if a clear indication of disinterest is shown by the women and the act of stalking continues, it is a crime under the law.

Stalking may also take the form of harassing telephone calls, computer communications, writing letters etc. or it can also happen on an online platform when a man monitors and harasses a woman on the internet, email or any other form of electronic communication. The act of stalking as of today, is a cognizable and bailable offence with a punishment up to three years and fine for the first conviction and five years and fine for the second conviction.

GENDER-NEUTRAL POLICIES AND PRACTICES AT WORKPLACE

The sexually unbiased arrangement at working environment is picking up hugeness everywhere throughout the world and India isn't a special case for it. The Indian business is continually concocting numerous inventive ladies strengthening approaches and practices like procuring more ladies workers; building up ladies well disposed workplace and so on. Be that as it may, today numerous associations have understood the requirement for creating sexual orientation unbiased arrangements and practices at work spot. The theory of sexual equity is to support such culture which isn't discriminative towards ladies; it is one which accommodates sexual orientation correspondence and huge open doors for ladies movement at work spot. Numerous activities that are proposed to help ladies representatives additionally observed to be all around adequately working out for men moreover. In this manner strategies and rehearses which were at first detailed remembering ladies' needs were later observed to be valuable crosswise over the two sexual orientations.

Gender neutrality is primarily about fairness and equality to all despite their background. It is a part of wider societal change that is meant to reveal the mechanisms of social injustice and to help with implementation of true equality in all respects. But gender neutrality is not an attempt to remove gender from people. Even it does not mean that denying the differences between women and men but rather about realizing the differences between them and the implications of these differences on their life time opportunities.

Gender neutral workplace means creating an environment that enables both women and men to perform. The workplace environment should be such that where all employees irrespective of their gender must be treated in the same manner; they do not feel inferior, superior, less important or more important than others at any time. They should get the same attention and the same space and time in the work environment.

<u>Socio-Economic set up in India</u>

Women in India were deprived of many things for quite a long time. During the past fifty decades, the socio-economic set up prevailed in India excluded women from many activities.

A woman who is not encouraged by her family to study and work, for instance, will not even enter the workplace and therefore will not contribute to either social change or the economy.

India is witnessing the confluence of dynamic forces such as liberalization, identity politics, religious tension and threats to national security etc. These forces have transpired into new challenges for the country thus prompting India to redefine its social norms. India while redefining these social norms realized that if women are not included in this national discourse, any stability that arises will be understandably precarious. Women at workplace have suffered exploitation, discrimination and inequality in India from a very long time.

<u>Workplace practices</u>: Indian industry became conscious regarding the potentialities and capabilities of women employees thus focusing more organizational sensitivity to deal with women at workplace issues with effectiveness at the ground level complementing the various constitutional laws meant for women at workplace. India is still putting its efforts to bring the changes in the mind sets of the people in the society with regard to women and their capabilities. In spite of all these, gender mainstreaming is posing a greater challenge to the country. There are many reasons for the prevalence of the current scenario because the percentage of women employees working in a particular firm is found significantly low. This indicates that how far a company is actively

pursuing a gender neutral hiring process across various work categories and positions. Moreover the percentage of women employees at senior management positions is also found very marginal. Apart from the above aspects in Indian workplaces gender stereotyping is very much apparent. Hence India has to take a longway to see gender neutral workplaces.

<u>Self limiting notion of women</u>: These are the barriers which arise due to some personal traits of women which are not very much appreciated in business. Such traits like avoidance of risk, not being assertive, not showing much interest in building networks are presumed to be undesirable for business organizations. Another point to be understood here is many of these traits are not only imbibed by her from the society and from corporate culture, but also from women themselves. In fact, women often perceive certain traits in a negative fashion; very often women

stereotype certain traits as unfeminine and thus consider them undesirable.

Hence the glass ceiling effects certainly will be on women as long as she herself comes forward to pierce the glass ceiling and climb the career ladder. Therefore in India this self limiting notion of women itself is acting as a dilemma in creating gender neutral workplace policies in an organization.

Creating a gender neutral workplace is becoming one of the thrust areas for business organizations in specific and for the country in general. Hence there is an urgent need to probe deeply into this aspect by corporate India and to assess their internal company culture and practices. The business organizations may take all possible measures to nurture gender neutral cultures. The government has to recognize and encourage such business organizations that are taking an initiatives and conscious steps to follow best gender neutral practices at the workplace. The social agencies should also come forward to assist, suggest and support these organizations in building gender neutral workplaces.

Gender Inequality[32]

Gender inequality is the question here. The reality of gender inequality in India, origin of gender inequality and how to deactivate it are discussed in this chapter.

This starts with the state of gender based inequality in the modern India. It presents some facts and figures representing the inequality practiced in India and its comparison with other Asian and Western countries.

The effects of the diversified culture and differences on the inequality in general are explained first.

The origin of the inequality and the effect of modern technologies in controlling the gender in population are briefly described. The route to the

---

[32] Christine E. Bose, University of Singapore

present scenario is explained to show the importance and influence of the origin of the problem and India's cultural background. The different areas where the inequality is felt and problems they face in each of those areas are explained. The strategies and initiatives being done by different groups and society in general are described to show the progress happening in India to reduce the problem of gender inequality.

Right off the bat, the truth of sexual orientation disparity in India is exceptionally intricate and differentiated, on the grounds that it is available in numerous ways, numerous fields and numerous classes. Fields like instruction, work openings, where men are continuously favored over ladies. Think about the case – a young lady taking confirmation in mechanical designing. Doesn't it sound somewhat ungainly on the grounds that it's constantly viewed as a man's field.

The sexual orientation imbalance looked by ladies was so much that numerous ladies guaranteed may god offer children to all. This is a reality and India has seen sexual orientation imbalance from its initial history because of its financial and religious practices that brought about a wide hole between the situation of people in the general public. Unmistakably, at that point sexual orientation holes that are boundless in access to fundamental rights, access to and control of assets, in monetary openings and furthermore in power and political voice are an obstruction to advancement.

Secondly, the origin of this gender inequality has always been the male dominance. At least in India, a woman still needs the anchor of a husband and a family. Their dominating nature has led women to walk with

their head down. It was all practiced from the beginning and is followed till date. In the case of woman's reservation in parliament , the opposing party believes that women are born to do household work and manage kids, and not to corrupt the country by taking hold over politics. Here, just as women's domestic work is undervalued, so are their skills in the world of employment. Most are concentrated in the poorly-paid, low skilled women's sectors of the economy.

The popular interpretations of Hindu mythology have very fixed views on how women should behave; things like being obedient and being a good housewife and mother. In the Ramayana, Ram is a model for how men should act and Sita is the model for women. Unfortunately, these play a part in perpetuating sexism and violence against women in India today.

If we focus on Hindu mythology, because 80% of Indians are Hindus and even non-Hindus are impacted by it, the religions in India view women in a similar light; they are not allowed to be independent. In some ways, these attitudes are used to justify violence against women. They blame the woman by saying she didn't behave like Sita. If she did, she would be fine.

In India, a sex-selection phenomenon has been in place since the 1980s, with men born during this period now at marriageable age. Then the urbanization since the 1990s where a lot of families and men have moved to cities to look for work. People are much wealthier but at the same time there's pressure to produce sons as an heir, so educated, wealthy families are now more likely to have sex selection. All these factors are coming to play and creating this toxic mixture, which has turned violence against women into a bigger issue today.

India's social structure is a unique blend of diverse religions, cultures and racial groups with the great religion of the world, viz, the Hindus, the Muslims, the Christians, etc, are found here. The 18 major literary languages, apart from numerous other languages and dialects adds to it. This leads to a striking diversity between various communities and groups in kinships and marriages rites, customs, inheritance and modes of living. Diversity is also seen in the pattern of rural as well as urban settlements, community life, cultural and social behaviour as also in the institutional framework.

In the ancient India women were held in high esteem and the the position of a woman in the Vedas and the Upanishads was that of a mother (maata) or goddess (Devi). In the Manusmriti, woman was considered as a precious being and in the early Vedic age, girls were looked after with care.

Then practice of polygamy deteriorated the status of woman and in the medieval period, the practices of purdha system, dowry and sati came into being. With the passage of time, the status of woman was lowered.

After the development of science and technology, female foeticide is being practiced on a large scale.

In many parts of India, women are viewed as an economic liability despite contribution in several ways to our society and economy. The crime graph against women is increasing at an alarming rate. The condition of an Indian widow is quite deplorable. At home, the woman's contribution towards home as a housewife is not recognized. Domestic Violence, Rape, Sexual Exploitation, molestation, eve-teasing, forced prostitution, sexual harassment at work places etc are a common affair today and in some cases its too tragic that it gets the global attention.

The major reasons for this inequality are identified as the need of a male heir for the family, huge dowry, continued financial support to girl child, poverty , domestic violence, farming as major job for poor and the caste system.

Features of Inequality

At work, this difference is noticeable through an alternate workplace for ladies , unequal wages, undignified treatment, inappropriate behavior, higher working hours, commitment in unsafe ventures, word related dangers, working generally twice the same number of hours as men and an about 27 level of ladies are accounted by unpaid exercises.

Brutality against ladies is likewise noticeable in India which prompts like clockwork a sexual provocation happening, at regular intervals a lady seized and like clockwork a lady is singed for share.

What's more, by the pre quarter of revealed, assaults include young ladies younger than 16 years. At regular intervals a lady is attacked and at regular intervals an assault occur.

Poor health care is another attitude towards women which makes them neglected during illness, recognition of illness by herself, health services as a last resort and reluctance to be examined by male doctors.

Lack of education in women has lead to poor literacy leading to gender gap in literacy rate and no higher education.

Economic constraints are also imposed to women in India by keeping them as dependents , no equal property rights (as against law) , loans of men is paid back by women , economic uncertainty and denial in inheritance of properties to orphaned / deserted.

Discriminative socialization process is another aspect of inequality towards women which leads to customary practices, more involvement in household activities only (boys not allowed), restricted to play ,

isolation, separation in schools and public places and restrictions to move freely. Detrimental cultural practices like after marriage husbands dominating the family , dominance from In-laws family , members , never or rarely considered for any decision making, limitations in continuing relationships with brothers , sisters , relatives, child or early marriage, patriarchal attitudes and not able to continue girl or boy friendship after marriage are also contributing factor to the inequality.

Strategies for advancement of women should be higher literacy, more formal education, greater employment opportunity. In education it needs to be reducing primary and secondary dropout of female child. In post literacy, the basic literacy skills at speaking, reading, and writing and problem solving shall be imparted.

Women learners should educate their children which further enhances social advancement.

In job opportunities there shall be reservation or expenditure or provision of services or special provisions. In governance all rights and all legal measures should be available for women's protection and support.

Human rights education , know how to take control of their circumstance , help to achieve their own goals, helping themselves, enhancing their quality of life and motivating for lobbying or advocacy are also enablers for their advancement.

Collaborators such as NGO, INGOs, NPOs, SHGs, CBOs , policy makers, local leaders , information disseminators ,health care providers , teachers and family members should help in the social advancement of women.

India need to deactivate the gender Inequality. The needs of the day are trends where girls are able not only to break out of the culturally determined patterns of employment but also to offer advice about career possibilities that look beyond the traditional list of jobs. It is surprising that in spite of so many laws, women still continue to live under stress and strain. To ensure equality of status for our women we still have miles to go.

153

Man and Woman are like two wheels of a carriage. The life of one without the other is incomplete

MISUSE OF GENDER SPECIFIC LAWS

The women protective laws have been enacted keeping in view the deplorable condition of women in the Indian society due to the subjection of women to discrimination and exploitation. The result of the women empowerment movements and women rights activists primarily resulted in a number of reforms for women along with some gender specific stringent provisions in favor of women. The provisions for women's protection stand justified on the pretext of the condition of women in old times as well as the crimes committed against them. However there has been a sharp rise in the misuse of these provisions against men. Men are moreover not provided protection for similar offences under law.

How can it be assumed that domestic violence can only be committed against a woman in the household?

Or how can only a woman be sexually harassed at a workplace or elsewhere? Or can it only be a woman who can get sexually assaulted and raped?

If the wife has the right to protect herself from cruelty by her husband then why not husband has the same right against his wife?

If a woman can seek protection under rape law why can't a man seek protection under it?

Where does the right under Article 14 disappear while enacting such provisions?

The laws relating to these offences and a few more like dowry provide immense power to women against men. This provides unjustified power in the hands of women many of who misuse them and jeopardize the life of men and their families.

The cause of men is completely neglected by the law by not providing them any recourse. There are special legislations for women to deal with almost every issue that concerns them like maintenance, protection from sati, domestic violence, dowry, harassment, etc, sadly all these provisions are blatantly misused by some.

 With the advancement in society and development of civilization the conditions are not the same as it were earlier. For instance women were treated with cruelty by their husband and his relatives as the position of women was weak, they were not empowered. But today where a woman stands on an equal footing with man there remains no difference. Both men and women can inflict cruelty which is of course not something gender specific, a wife can also inflict cruelty on her husband and in that case there is no recourse available to the husband. The legislative bend in the favor of women makes it worse for men as taking advantage of these provisions women conveniently get away with it. It is not uncommon then that using these provisions as a threat the women actually inflict cruelty upon their husband. Cruelty is a behavior which is exhibited by humans and not "male" or "female" specifically. Be it male or female, one can inflict cruelty upon the other.

The basic objective behind a law is the protection of people but what when it actually becomes a means of threatening and terror? A large number of complaints are filed under the said provisions which are based on false accusations and merely for personal gains and motives. Such misuse of these laws not only deprives the justice to real victims who seek protection under law, by flooding the courts with cases but also brings disharmony in the society and hampers peace. Additionally also jeopardizing men.

The Supreme Court, in a relatively recent case, **Sushil Kumar Vs. Union of India**[33] held that object of the provision is prevention of dowry menace. But as has been rightly contended by the petitioner that many instances have come to light where the

---

[33] Writ Petition (civil) 141 of 2005

complaints are not bonafide and have been filed with oblique motive. In such cases acquittal of the accused does not in all cases wipe out the ignomy suffered during the prior to trial.

Similarly in **Preeti Gupta Vs. State of Jharkhand**[34] Hon'ble Supreme Court has observed that it is a matter of common experience that most of these complaints under section 489A, IPC are filed in the heat of the moment over trivial issues without proper deliberation. Allegations of harassment by relatives, being at faraway places, should be scrutinized with great care. Criminal trial leads to immense suffering for all concerned. Even ultimate acquittal in the trial may not e able to wipe out the deep scars of suffering of ignomity. It is high time that the legislatures must take into consideration the pragmatic realities and make suitable changes in the existing law.

---

[34] AIR 2010 SC 3363

The gender specific laws for the protection of women have actually provided them with legislative superiority over men. The potential of the misuse of these provisions is huge and the number of such cases of misuse is on a rampant increase. How easy would it be then to use these provisions against any man as a means of seeking vengeance or extort money? The fact that these provisions have been used for meeting such ends is not neglected but now it has become a grave issue.

There are numerous cases where ulterior motive guide the false allegations against men, it appears to be the easiest way for a woman to file charges and get want they want. Most of the cases of blackmailing come to the forefront where men are blackmailed on the context of being accused of such offences. They are blackmailed and extorted money or other favors.

Even if the false accusations are proved to be false in the court and allegations are set aside the reputation of the accused gets tarnished and the accused and his family face the stigma that such accusations result into. Innocent families undergo victimization and emotional trauma. There have been cases of suicide by men which is driven by the fear of their families being drawn into the entire ordeal. The men in our country are facing such mental torture and are being drawn into false accusation everyday with an alarming rate of increase in such number.

SUFFERER? BOTH MEN AND WOMEN

Hasn't men been treated with injustice over centuries like women have been? The question that is rising up is how, right? After all men have been considered superior to women in all ways, they have been bestowed with the responsibility of looking after and earning for their family, of being strong, of dealing with all societal affairs.

The answer is that they too have suffered injustice by being denied the right to choose the way they live. The society has always held back a woman from entering the mainstream as household has been the arena she is supposed to be concerned with, similarly men too have been forced to work and earn and deal with the worldly affairs without any choice.

The society has never considered the fact that the two are humans and the two of them have been equally bestowed with the same emotions and capabilities and confining them to roles on the basis of their sex is an injustice to both.

Men have been considered to be strong and have never been allowed to depict any emotions. They have never been allowed to grieve or express anything they feel which in the eyes of the society would stain the label of 'strong'. Growing up in the same society we all must have observed how even at the greatest losses of loved ones the male members of the family do not even shed a tear. How they are made to undergo very trial of life without expressing how much they are hurt in the process.

Men have undergone mental torture over time immemorial when each man has been burdened with the responsibilities and obligation to pursue the conventional fields which primarily concerned affairs that dealt with outside world. Haven't you witnessed even today in a family the son is always raised to stand upto the expectations of the family, to earn when he grows up and to pursue only that which is thought to be glorious to the family's reputation. Fields like cooking, art, designing, etc which were considered to be household affairs are not allowed to be pursued even if the son wants to.

The challenges for men have always been neglected by the society. We do accept how unconventional fields are not allowed by the society to be pursued by women, we do accept how they are forced to limit themselves to the four walls of the household but we always fail to accept any injustice which is face by men vice versa.

The greatest injustice to them being the incapacitation to express their emotions, which leads to pent up emotions and a lot of mental problems as a result of the same.

The problem is that the society has been unjust to both the genders by defining roles and limiting them to confine to those. The fact that both the genders are human beings has been forgotten. The biological differences has formed the sole determining factor of the lives which they are to live ahead irrespective of the choices they want to make, irrespective of the capacities they possess, irrespective of the fact that they as human are born free and not with some predefined role to play after their birth.

We often say that being a woman is tough as she has her struggles as a woman along with the problems that the society creates for her but has anyone wondered that being a man can be tough too?

Men have to live by the expectations of conforming to the ideals of 'real manhood', which revolve around some stereotypes which have no logical base behind them. For a simple instance a boy who does not like going out and playing outdoor has something seriously wrong as he is defying the stereotype that boys go out and play. He can be more interested in staying indoors and reading and that is when he does not fit in the ideals. Or let's suppose an adolescent who is not much inclined in going gym is targeted over and over again with questions as to his masculinity. Such irrational stereotypes do actually exist in the society.

All these find their base in patriarchy; it not just affects women but also men in ways numerous.

A man who lets his wife participate equally in major decisions or lets her take her decisions is labeled to be unmanly. He has to earn and pay bills, he has to take all decisions, he has to be dominant in all ways, he has to provide security, an earning man can marry a non-earning woman but a non-earning man is unfit to marry an earning woman or any woman for that matter, he cannot speak about his emotions etc. and where he deviates from any of these standards then questions are raised on his manhood.

The society does not let both men and women live at peace who rightly consider them as human beings first and their choice to live by the same. They are compelled to abide by the norms and roles created by the society.

Patriarchy has had a damaging effect not just on women but also on men and we need to recognize this fact at the earliest to address the problem.

Gender equality has actually not been addressed because the inequalities have not been even recognized. The gender roles should be put an end to. Why is there a need to define human beings into two different genders? The term sex takes into account the biological differences and that is sufficient. There has not to be any differentiation on the roles assigned.

We need to learn that we are human beings and should endeavor to be compassionate and good human beings rather than being masculine or feminine.

CONCLUSION

India as a developing nation has been taking up reforms and measures with respect to social, economic, political and cultural development. It is striving to eliminate all that hinders its progress and the progress of each and every citizen of the nation. Amidst such endeavors with all noble pursuits it becomes our duty to shed false beliefs and contribute equally to its development.

The people of India on 26th January 1950 adopted, enacted and gave themselves the Indian Constitution. The preamble which is the key to the constitution and introduces the basic structure and principles of the constitution states that India has to secure to all its citizens "EQUALITY of status and of opportunity". It is this equality that we have been talking about. Gender- equality in all forms and treatment without any biasness be it for men or women, equality means both genders at par.

Going through the history of the structure of the society and the role of men and women in it, a clear inference can be drawn as to the reasons why the society is facing present day problems. First the apparent subjugation and oppression of women and the denial of any rights to them and then with the uprising in the voice against such oppression the interests and protection of men receding in the background.

Like most of the issues which any society faces the one linked with gender inequality is also a result of the psychological being of the people. It is the false beliefs which the people clung to which give rise to problems. Earlier and even today majority of the population believes in the superiority of men over women which results in offences against women and the denial of men being victim to any such offence.

Even if laws are formulated which would provide protection to men as well the condition would not really improve because men would at the first hand not report any cases due to the same reasons which have already been discussed earlier. Likewise despite a number of legislative reforms and punitive measures against any crime against women the condition of women hasn't really improved much; in fact the nature of crimes has become more heinous.

What actually will provide a solution to all problems then if it cannot be resolved by any act of Parliament? A solution which is the most benefitting comes only when the very root of the problem is struck. Analyzing the root of all the gender specific problems is not hard as we know it is the society only which has actually defined the term gender. The conferment of different roles and the belief that the two opposite sex are not at par is the very root which needs to be targeted.

The age old beliefs need to be completely shed by each and every individual who comprises the society. State monitoring if would have resolved problems then the problems would have ceased to exist at all the very day any legislation to address that problem came into force. What is required is a change in the beliefs of the people, the shedding of the stereotypes held by them surrounding femininity and masculinity. After all the legislature is formed by the people who are a part of the same society and represent the interest of the people who elected them which again is a part of the society. No member of parliament who participates in the formulation of laws is descended down from heaven or any alien land. Therefore there is a change in the mindset of the people which is required. Everything would then fall in the right place.

We need to realize that there had been some practices which were not for the good of the society and were based on false beliefs and therefore with time such practices were given up by the people gradually. With the changing times the nature of patriarchy has become mild but has not lost its essence and existence and still continues its hold in almost every Indian household. With such tight hold of patriarchy on the minds of the people the problems which the females have been facing continue and what is more threatening is that some new issues considering men have arisen too. A practice which favored men has now put them in peril to suffice.

We talked about a number of issues like sexual harassment, adultery, rape, domestic violence, dowry deaths etc and it would not be a mistake to say that somewhere it is patriarchal values which have been responsible for the same either directly or indirectly. For all the offences against women it is the idea of them being treated as lifeless objects meant to serve men. And for all the negation of the need for protection of men from such offences in the present day again the idea of male superiority over women which makes it something that is not considered possible.

The nation has protested for the rights of women as they have faced oppression for centuries and continue to face it in some form or the other. The government has too protected them in all ways possible. The oppression still continues because the people have not undergone a change in the beliefs which they continue to hold. The perpetrators of such offences still hold the same beliefs of subordinate status of females. Adding to this, the perpetrators escape punishment because somewhere the protectors of law are also not descended down from heaven and are people from the same society which holds the same beliefs.

The issue has been gaining ground is of the fact that the laws which protect women are being misused by some for personal gains. That becomes an entirely different subject to discuss as the laws have always been used and misused.

What has been being neglected by all is the fact that men are not provided any protection under law when it comes to any sexual offences, domestic violence, dowry offences, etc They are humans too and are equally vulnerable at the hands of the same or opposite sex and are yet deprived from any protection. This being due to the fact that they have been considered an epitome of superiority, their gender has been considered to be superior and stronger. This results in absolute denial of the fact that any man can be a victim to any such offence.

The grave injustice which is being meted out to them is not taken into consideration at all. At least the fact that a woman can be a victim to an offence and the law which provides her protection do exist but in the case of men there is absolutely no recourse they can resort to in the face of any such offence.

Where would a man who is raped seek justice or protection? The law does not recognize it, the society would mock him in face, his own friends and family belong to the same society holding the same beliefs that no such thing can happen. He is only made to suffer trauma for the rest of his life as he has to remain silent and not even raise his voice because there is no acceptance for a man who falls a victim to a woman.

Isn't the condition of this man even worse than a woman? To say the least, the law protected her and she could seek protection under it but the man cannot. The number of crimes against men has been rising but the same has not been reported and there is no demand by the society for reforms in that direction.

The need of the hour is to consider both the genders at par as human beings. The labels of 'superior' and 'inferior' need to be discarded at the earliest. The roles defined to them based on their sex need to be done away with. It is not just women now but also men who are being affected by the discrimination.

To establish a society with equality to all irrespective of any difference as to caste, creed, gender, sex, etc is what the Constitution upholds. It is our responsibility as the citizens of India that we bring about a change in our beliefs and start considering everyone as fellow human beings. Only then a change is plausible. Laws have been formulated and will continue to be formulated addressing several issues which concern the society and that is vital too but change can only be expected when each one of us resolve to bring about a change in the mindset.

There is an urgent need for the laws to be gender neutral and not gender specific. Be it any subject matter that the law deals with, both men and women have the right to equal protection. The specific nature of the statutes with regard to gender has lately resulted in the greater misuse of those statutes as well as left the opposite gender vulnerable at the hands of the one being protected.

There is no rationale which supports the gender specific nature of the provisions except the plea that the number of victims generally belongs to that gender and that too cannot serve as justifiable on the part of the legislature which has a duty to protect every citizen taking into account any slightest possibility too. The duty of the state is to protect all its citizens and even to deter them from committing any offence against any other citizen and that implies that the citizen can belong to any gender.

Thus India needs gender- neutral laws on every subject to establish the true meaning of gender equality in the society. Gender equality isn't a concept peculiar to the upliftment of women, it is on the other hand establishing a just and fair order in the society where both the genders enjoy equal status and opportunity.

PERSONAL OPINION

Men are being treated as Just ATM Machines & sperm donors. They have just responsibilities but no rights. They are not being treated as humans.

Men have no dignity or modesty. Indian system, society and judiciary thinks that a crime like rape and outraging the modesty can be only committed by men. Women are treated as saints.

Society thinks men can't be raped. Because according to them the urge for sex in only in men.

They think only Men are the perpetrators of a heinous crime like rape and stalking.

In Indian circumstances, an assault of a woman is more widespread due to the strong influence of the feudal and patriarchal nature of the society. Empowering women and their safety is a big concern for the justice system and therefore is at the forefront of all legislation. That being said, when men themselves accept the fact that their counterparts also face such assault and educate and spread awareness compelling legislators to take note, that can act as a catalyst for a change in the mindset of law makers.

Today, men and boys are routinely portrayed as idiotic, pathetic, uncouth and inferior creatures who are constantly in need of rescue by their "superior" wives, girlfriends or female relatives who are all set to overhaul them.

The society considers kicking, punching and slapping men as acceptable and even laudable behavior on the part of women and girls.

Ridiculing male sexuality is considered harmless entertainment, and the few men and boys who protest are considered peevish and lacking in humor.

When I[35] was growing up, I noticed that every time a woman or girl suffered injustice, insult or attack (real or perceived), in the hands of a male, someone would promptly ask the offender, "Don't you have a mother or sister?" Men and boys in India are constantly reminded of their mother, sister and daughter no matter what another woman is pained about.

I eagerly wait for the day when women will be reminded of their fathers, brothers, sons, partners, male colleagues and friends every time they cause, commit or witness injustice, insult or injury against a man. I look forward to the day when men will shed their silence, stand up and thwart the slightest attack on the sexuality, dignity and modesty of men.

Martin Luther King Jr. once said that "human progress is neither automatic

---

[35] Udit

nor inevitable; it requires the tireless exertions and passionate concern of dedicated individuals"

Human beings are violent and aggressive. Women are not an exception to it.

Yes, you read that right. The law in India is very sexist.

Ladies, an erection does not equate consent.

There is no room for adult male victims in Indian legal system.

Make rape laws gender neutral.

It discriminates against men. Here's how laws for Sexual Harassment or Rape: After the amendment bill passed in 2013, the moment a woman files an FIR (first information report) against a man, the police will arrest him.

Male rape is more common than we think. We need to de-gender our legal definition of rape. The conversation around male rape doesn't take away from the conversation around violence against women, our compassion should neither be finite nor gender segregated.

I do believe in gender equality and women empowerment, but women empowerment should occur through education and financial independence. Not by giving them a weapon against men, a weapon that can be used without repercussions.

Do some women/girls misuse the laws made for their protection?

They probably do, although they shouldn't but, they still do. Do all women misuse the law?

Absolutely not.

International Men's Day, marked on November 19 does not have the visibility or marketing acumen of Women's Day, "but is growing in significance every year." In 1946, a UN Commission on Women's Rights was set up, which has been dealing with the enforcement of women's rights and interests ever since. A UN Commission on Men's Rights has not yet been established by the United Nations. One could list at great length the many problems that afflict men today, including the male suicide epidemic, the paucity of resources for male victims of domestic violence and the falling behind of young men and boys in education. However there is one fundamental factor related to all these problems that men encounter: there is a lack of mainstream acceptance of systemic men's issues which is compounded by the absence of male advocacy groups with a broad remit to make the case at political level and the level of the media.

Also there is no National Men's Council, State funded or otherwise, to offer a counterbalance to the prevailing narrative about men being the perennially privileged class in society with no serious, systemic issues requiring advocacy.

Historically, men have had no issues organising as trade unionists, or in groups dedicated to protesting against inequalities faced by minorities based on their race or sexuality. This is not the case for men's advocacy.

Such advocates are typically met with contempt when attempting to add a discussion of men's issues to the national dialogue on gender equality. Such negative attitudes may well be a factor in why many men are so reluctant to come forward.

Society and its power relations, norms, and values are changing. Men have started sharing their agony, torture, and harassment by women/spouses. It is time to recognize their problem as a social and public health issue and develop appropriate strategies and interventions. They are no longer stronger than women. They need help in crisis and family violence: Particularly violence by spouse is a crisis. Male victims of violence can be saved/helped through appropriate intervention such as recognition of violence against men by women as a public health issue; helpline for the male victims of violence; and education, awareness, and legal safeguards.

Women can be both abusers and victims. Same applies to men.

Everyone has a level of privilege and oppression - the levels just vary according to factors such as: sex, able-bodiedness, country, skin colour, sexual orientation, gender identity and socio-economical status. No one is asking you to apologise for your privileges - we're asking you to acknowledge them. That's it. Recognition and understanding of ones advantages and disadvantages and how they relate to other people is the first step to changing how society places value on people.

Happy reading!